CAREERS

F O R

TRAVEL
BUFFS

& Other
Restless Types

CAREERS
FOR
TRAVEL
BUFFS
& Other
Restless Types

Paul Plawin

VGM Career Horizons
a division of *NTC Publishing Group*
Lincolnwood, Illinois USA

Library of Congress Cataloging-in-Publication Data

Plawin, Paul, 1938–
  Careers for travel buffs & other restless types / Paul Plawin.
    p.   cm. — (VGM careers for you series)
  ISBN 0-8442-8109-3. — ISBN 0-8442-8127-1 (pbk.) : $8.95
  1. Vocational guidance.   2. Travel.   I. Title.   II. Title:
Careers for travel buffs and other restless types.   III. Title:
Travel buffs.   IV. Series.
HF5381.P655   1991
331.7'02—dc 20   91-23476
                                                                 CIP
                                                                  AC

1996 Printing

Published by VGM Career Horizons, a division of NTC Publishing Group.
© 1992 by NTC Publishing Group, 4255 West Touhy Avenue,
Lincolnwood (Chicago), Illinois 60646-1975 U.S.A.
Manufactured in the United States of America.

    6 7 8 9 0 VP 9 8 7 6 5 4

Contents

About The Author

*P*aul Plawin has been a journalist and writer for 30 years. He began his career as a newspaper reporter, then moved to magazines and spent more than 23 years as an editor with *Southern Living, Better Homes & Gardens,* and *Changing Times, Kiplinger's Personal Finance Magazine.* Mr. Plawin covered court trials, police raids, and the military in his newspaper days. As a magazine editor, he wrote about subjects ranging from small business and career strategies to travel and leisure life-styles. Mr. Plawin is married, has two children, and now runs an editorial services and video production firm in Falls Church, Virginia.

Foreword

For my part, I travel not to go anywhere, but to go. I travel for travel's sake.
The great affair is to move.   Robert Louis Stevenson.

Traveling is exciting, enlightening, and experiential. As Robert
Louis Stevenson so aptly put it, travel is all these things because
of movement—because of the ability to change a setting or
environment through motion. The opportunities for travel and
careers involving travel are limitless since movement facilitates
communication and, in turn, the exchange of ideas, information, and business.

People travel for many reasons—whether it be for business or
pleasure—and more and more are doing it. The size of the travel
industry is indicative of travel's importance to our society and its
popularity since it amassed $327 billion for the nation last year
as U.S. citizens took more than 1.3 billion trips.

Travel, by virtue of movement and the communication and
contact it produces, acts as a peace ambassador, an educator, and
a market for ideas and cultures. Anyone involved in traveling,
knowingly or unknowingly, functions as a diplomat, teacher,
student, and marketer.

Aside from these abstractions, travel is fun, and many careers
allow employees the opportunity to do so, which is often mutu-
ally beneficial to both parties. This book provides an excellent

glimpse into the careers, both within and outside the travel industry, which enable employees to visit and experience the world. Take advantage of the great opportunities and joys that come with travel by making it part of your job and life.

Edward R. Book
President
Travel Industry Association of America

Introduction

I like to travel—always have. I loved Boy Scout camping trips when I was a kid. For someone who grew up where there were sidewalks and apartment buildings, these excursions into the wilderness (now probably suburban residential developments) were exhilarating. Those junky looking country stores we explored on our overnight hikes were exotic bazaars where we dug into our pockets for change to buy Bazooka bubble gum, cinnamon hot hardball candies and wine-soaked crook cigars that we smoked surreptitiously when the scoutmasters were out of sight.

Every summer my family would visit the relatives 350 miles distant. I always looked forward to these trips—despite memories of getting carsick when we drove too far in the '38 Chevy. During our vacation, we'd manage a side-trip or two. Because my dad and his brother were interested in Civil War history, we roamed the old battlefields at Petersburg and Antietam and Gettysburg. My memories of these rumpled fields and redoubts are still vivid.

My first trip to New York City was on one of these family excursions. I remember going to the observation deck in the Empire State Building and being on a tour bus where someone pointed out men sleeping on the sidewalk as typical scenery in the Bowery. And dining at the Automat, where you looked at hot meals, cold salads, rolls, and desserts in individual little windows. You put change in the coin slots to open the window and extract what you had selected. They had nothing like this back home.

When I went off to college, I made friends with people from other parts of the country; we shared stories and dreams, and my horizons expanded. We used to hitchhike to other college towns or to the big city. To be stranded from time to time, alongside a highway, seemingly in the middle of nowhere—that was an experience to be relished, a sort of macho thing.

In our own cars, we made road trips to all sorts of places. Once a friend and I tooled through the countryside for two or three days just to find things we had read about—like a particular beach or the world's largest chair in the square of a North Carolina furniture factory town. Those were great trips.

For a time I daydreamed about shipping out on a freighter to see the world. I'd leave the ship when I got someplace I really wanted to see, and live there for a while. Who knows, someday I might return to America—wise beyond my years. I'd be an experienced world traveler. Ah, dreams.

I married a girl from out of town, so I had to travel to see her when we were courting. Fortunately, she liked the idea of traveling, too. When we got married, we went to Nassau, in the Bahamas, on our honeymoon. It was our first tropical island. Nassau was just like the travel brochures showed it—sparkling, clear water; white, powdery sand; blue sky and blazing sun. I got so sunburned by our third day there that I was walking like an old man. But what a time we had. We arrived home with just enough change in our pockets to call someone to come and pick us up at the airport.

A Travel Career

As much as I liked to travel, I didn't really connect it to my first job as a newspaper reporter. There were some brushes with wanderlust in those days—when I'd go aboard a foreign flag ship to interview the captain for a feature story, or encounter a story subject who had traveled. Once I interviewed Gene "Wrong Way" Corrigan when he visited friends in my town. He was quite old. I barely knew of the air travel exploits on which his renown was based, but Corrigan still told his story with a crackle to it.

After a couple years of newspapering, I got a job with a big-time magazine. We moved to a new and bigger city. I began traveling in my work. Finally I was able to combine my love of travel and my job. Often my wife would go along as I gathered stories across the landscape. We loved it, and it was the start of my career as a travel writer and editor.

Eventually I took a job as the travel editor for *Better Homes & Gardens* magazine in Des Moines, Iowa. That was in 1967. We've been traveling ever since, and I've been writing about travel ever since. I have also written about jobs and careers over the years, primarily with *Changing Times, Kiplinger's Personal Finance Magazine.* So in this book, I have the opportunity to combine the two subjects.

Jobs for Travel Buffs

What you will find herein is a little bit of the good and the bad about more than a score of careers in which travel plays an important part. Although some of these career fields are small, with relatively few workers, all of them are open to anyone who will put in the time and effort to prepare for the field.

When we think travel careers, we tend to think first of jobs in transportation—with airlines, railroads, cruise lines, and shipping companies—and of travel agents. But as you will learn here, you don't have to be a pilot, railroad engineer, ship captain, bus driver, or ticket salesperson in order to travel in your work. There are several dozen kinds of jobs, for people with a variety of skills, in which travel is an important part of the work routine.

There are also some traveling jobs—such as those of astronauts and rock stars—that few people can hope to land. But who knows, if space exploration expands as rapidly in the next century as it has in the twentieth, thousands of travel buffs with every work skill known to society could be needed for spaceship flight crews and orbiting space platforms.

In each chapter that follows, you will find a description of what a field is like and what kind of jobs it supports—including the work and where travel fits into the routine. If you're interested, you can read on to discover exactly how to get into that field, what the typical pay scales are, the training and background you must have, and where you can get more detailed information about the career field and preparing for it.

CHAPTER ONE

The Travel Industry

Travel Agents

Nearly everyone who travels may eventually turn to a travel agent for help in planning a trip. Travel agents sell travel. They make recommendations about destinations you should visit and how you should get there. They also make your transportation, hotel, and tour package reservations for you. After paying the bill, all you have to do is get to the airport or train station on time.

Of course, buying travel is a bit more complicated than buying a new pair of shoes, and it's a lot more expensive. The tab for a couple planning a two-week escorted tour in Europe can be in the $5,000 to $6,000 range. With that kind of purchase, good travel agents pride themselves on giving their clients lots of information and helpful advice. Especially for international travel, there is much to know about—customs regulations, passports, visa requirements, certificates of vaccination, currency exchange, and rules of the road for drivers.

Promotion

Travel agents can't just wait for those $6,000 customers to walk in with their checkbooks at the ready. Agents must know how to attract business and how to keep their clients coming back for pleasurable trips.

One way agents do this is by promoting their expert knowledge of the tourist destinations of the world and of the logistic and mechanical intricacies of travel. They have access to all sorts of published and computer-based sources of data on all elements of a trip—airline, train, and cruise line schedules and fares; availability of discounts; the range of hotel rates; package tour ingredients and prices; rental car deals; critical ratings of individual hotels and restaurants.

Travel agents often attend meetings where they can give slide shows or other presentations about their services to special interest groups, and they regularly call on businesses to solicit their business travel accounts.

The Daily Routine

The way travel agents acquire much of their knowledge is by taking trips. Nothing beats firsthand experience and observations. Airlines, cruise lines, hotel chains, and tour operators regularly host travel agents on familiarization trips ("fam" tours) where agents can check out itineraries and facilities they'll sell to their clients.

Agents often go on fam tours in the off season at popular travel destinations. There is more space available then and more time for them to look around. Also, in the prime travel season, travel agents are usually chained to their desks and computer consoles working out travel plans for their customers.

Travel agents regularly visit hotels, resorts, and restaurants to rate firsthand their comfort and cleanliness and the quality of the food and wine. They base their recommendations on their own travel experiences as well as those of colleagues and long-time clients. Traveling is also a way to learn about typical weather conditions, off-the- beaten-path restaurants, sight-seeing attractions, and recreation opportunities at destinations around the globe.

But even for travel agents, there is never enough time to travel. Most of their time is spent at their desks conferring with clients and completing the chain of paperwork that holds together a well-planned trip. Travel agents spend hours on the phone with tour operators and guides, and at the computer terminal punching in data to confirm your reservations and order your tickets.

Travel agents work everywhere. Many are self-employed. Few towns are too small to support a travel agent. About half the travel agents in the United States work from offices in suburban areas; 40 percent, in large cities; the rest in small towns and rural areas.

The trend now is for agencies to specialize in types of travel—business, cruises, adventure trips, personalized itineraries. Another trend is the growth of major travel agencies with lots of branch offices, particularly in major metropolitan areas. Because business travel represents steady and usually hefty sales, many travel agencies go out of their way to attract corporate clients.

Agencies that specialize in planning vacation trips are referred to as boutique agencies; they tend to be small and offer highly personalized service. Some agencies become "discounters." They give back some of the commission to their customers, offer little or no service other than ticket sales, and often operate only over the phone with nationwide 800 numbers.

Getting into the Business

Becoming a travel agent usually requires specialized training nowadays. Few agencies train people on the job. They'll normally refer you to one of the many vocational schools that offer three- to twelve-week courses for beginning travel agents.

With actual work experience, plus further study and examinations over 18 months, an agent can earn the coveted Certified Travel Counselor (CTC) designation from the Institute of Certified Travel Agents. Another mark of achievement in the field is a certificate of proficiency from the American Society of Travel Agents, which is awarded to agents who pass a three-hour exam.

A travel agent's job also requires the ability to work with computer databases and a head for basic business accounting and planning practices. Previous experience in the travel field is an asset. For example, some agents were previously airline reservations agents or ticketing agents.

An agent also needs good selling skills. Characteristics that help in this department are a pleasant personality, patience, and the ability to gain the confidence of clients. Agent-client trust is a key here. For potential clients, choosing a travel agent is like choosing a doctor or lawyer—once the agent's competence has been established, the choice often comes down to personal chemistry and trust. This is where the personality and integrity of an agent are major assets.

Personal travel experience is also an asset for an agent, since firsthand knowledge about destinations can help influence a client's travel plans, and the ability to continually steer clients to places and experiences they enjoy brings repeat business to an agent.

If you work for a travel agency, the agency will hold formal approvals from travel suppliers such as air and rail lines and rental car companies. Those approvals enable travel agents to draw commissions when they sell the products of those companies. To earn those approvals, an agency must demonstrate that it is financially and operationally sound and has been in business for a period of time. In several states, travel agents must also be licensed. The toughest aspect of becoming a self-employed travel agent, or opening a new agency, is operating successfully for long enough to win the approvals from key suppliers that allow you to earn commissions.

Your Future as a Travel Agent

Job opportunities for travel agents should grow much faster than average throughout the 1990s. The job openings will be created as new travel agencies open, existing agencies expand, and agents retire, and otherwise leave the field, and need to be replaced.

The rosy forecast for the field stems from the expectation that spending on travel will continue to increase significantly through the year 2000. This prediction is based on several factors. For one thing, the number of job openings in managerial, professional, specialty and sales representative occupations—those traveling salespeople and executives described elsewhere in this book—is projected to grow rapidly. And as business activity expands, so will business-related travel.

Also, as incomes rise, more people are expected to travel on vacations and to do so more frequently than in the past. Already many people take more than one vacation a year. Airfare deals and larger, more efficient planes have brought air travel within the budgets of more people than ever before. So growing numbers of travelers will seek travel agents to help them arrange their trips. American travel agents who organize tours for the growing number of foreign visitors to the United States will also prosper as this trend continues.

A note of caution: The travel industry is very sensitive to economic conditions. When the economy slumps, and people are pinched in the pocketbook, their travel plans are the first things to be put off in order to get through the economic hard times. So travel agencies often find that the volume of their business fluctuates and is dependent on the state of the economy as a whole.

Earnings and Benefits

Earnings of travel agents depend largely on commissions from their sale of travel products. Those who are employees of agencies may draw a base salary and receive some fringe benefits. According to one survey, salaries of travel agents, including commission, range from about $14,500 for beginners to $25,300 a year for experienced agents, with managers of agencies earning about $36,000.

The commission rate for domestic travel purchases—such as cruises, airplane tickets, hotels, package tours, and car rentals—is about 10 percent of total sales; for international travel elements, it's about 11 percent. A travel agent who sells you a $400 air ticket and a $2,100 tour package for a U.S. destination earns a total commission of $250.

Sometimes travel agents are asked to put together special itineraries. This may involve coordinating various air and ground transportation connections, placing international calls to make reservations at exclusive hotels, and offering other extraordinary services or arrangements. Travel agents may charge a service fee on top of their commission for the extra time and cost involved in making these special arrangements. Earnings of self-employed agents, of course, are totally dependent on commissions and service fees. When they are just starting out and don't yet have commission approval from airlines and car rental companies, self-employed agents must survive on commissions from suppliers who don't require formal approval. Such suppliers include cruise lines, hotels, and tour companies. So earnings for self-employed travel agents may be very low at the start.

As key sales agents for travel industry suppliers, travel agents usually get substantial discounts when they travel (up to 75% off on the cost of their transportation and accommodations). Sometimes they travel free as the guests of airlines, hotels, and destinations that want the agents to experience their services and products and recommend them to future clients.

For more information:

American Society of Travel Agents
1101 King Street
Alexandria, VA 22314

Association of Retail Travel Agents
1745 Jefferson Davis Highway, Suite 300
Arlington, VA 22202

Institute of Certified Travel Agents
148 Lindon Street
P.O. Box 56
Wellesley, MA 02181

Tour Guides

Do you have a keen sense of history? Do you love to share your
knowledge of the lore and legend of places with your friends and
colleagues? Are you a good "people person," able to mix with
folks of all types and have them look to you for direction? Have
you the unique ability to talk while walking backwards?

You do? Then you could be a tour guide.

Professional tour guides trace their craft to the eighteenth
century tradition of the European *cicerone* (after ancient Roman
orator and philosopher Cicero). The cicerone was the local
interpreter who explained the history and curiosities of a place
to visitors. The wealthy citizens who could travel the world
would seek appointments with the cicerone of a city or region to
learn everything about it—its history, architecture, culture,
commerce, and people. In this way, influential travelers from
distant places came to better understand one another's societies.
The efforts of cicerones helped civilize the world; suspicions and
other barriers between regions were lowered.

Today the cicerone is the professional tour guide. Actually,
the profession includes several types of guides: tour managers,
who escort and manage a group's travel on a multiday tour; tour
guides, who take people on sight-seeing excursions of more
limited duration; driver/guides, who both drive a tour motorcoach and provide narration en route, usually on local tours;
step-on guides, or city guides, who come aboard a touring motorcoach to provide expert information about their city; and do-
cents, usually volunteers, who lead tours of museums.

Tour guiding can be a glamorous life covering as many miles as you care to spend on the road each year. But those who make it their career find that this life also has its frustrations and shortcomings.

The Work

Edwin D. Farrell, a tour guide and chief executive of the Professional Guides Association of America, says there are many misconceptions about the field.

It isn't a continuous carefree journey throughout the world. It is shepherding 40 or so bus passengers around a town, state, or region of the world in all kinds of weather, tending to their various needs. Tour guides on multiday tours are on call 24 hours a day and must minister to passengers who need medical attention, have strayed from the group, get arrested by the local police, or have other problems that they expect their guide to at least help them solve. And to be successful, guides must perform these wonders with aplomb!

The occupation does offer many satisfactions. As a guide, you have the opportunity to meet people from all over the world. If you are a locally based guide, you become the official spokesperson and goodwill ambassador for a city, region, or the entire country to the travelers you serve. As the modern day cicerone, you can help bridge cultural differences as you explain sights and sounds to visitors on tour.

Travelers on group tours look to guides as educators. They want to learn about the places they visit, and they expect you to have authoritative answers to all their questions. Travelers also expect you to educate them in an entertaining manner. Of course, guides learn from their charges, too. Many guides tell of regularly receiving letters from passengers who have taken their tours. Veteran travelers have been known to book only tours that their favorite guides will be leading.

Guides must know about group dynamics in order to make sure each individual in a tour group is recognized in some way and is able to appreciate the trip and the guide's narrative. Of course, to survive in this field, a guide basically must like people. In addition, guides must be well educated, especially in history, geography, and civics. It helps if they have learned something about psychology, speech, and drama as well. Guides must base their narrative programs on solid research, including keeping up with current events in various locales. The most successful guides also possess specialized knowledge in certain subjects, such as art, architecture, archeology, and the like. Those who are fluent in foreign languages can earn higher fees.

Crisis management is also a skill professional guides must acquire. As the leader of a group of people on the road, a guide has to be able to cope with emergencies and contingencies that can rattle the untrained—a driver who becomes incapacitated, a fire on a motorcoach, the illness or death of a passenger, foul-ups involving hotel reservations and other travel arrangements. Guides routinely have to deal with maps, itineraries, and timetables; airline check-in procedures; early morning bag pulls from hotel corridors. To run a route, they need to know about traffic patterns on tour routes, availability of motorcoach parking at various destinations, procedures for entering tourist attractions.

For a guide, it pays to have a good sense of humor, an outgoing personality, honesty and ethics, diplomacy and tact. Good health also is important—to avoid becoming physically run down by the pace of travel (on your feet for hours at a time, eating on the run, infrequent restroom stops). And here's where the facility to walk backwards while talking comes in! That's a situation most tour guides frequently find themselves in while leading their charges through yet another lavish garden or restored frontier fort. Guides also often find themselves riding backwards—as they must stand at the front of their motorcoach and address travelers about sights that are ahead of passengers, but behind the guide.

Getting into the Business

Farrell says it can be tough to get off to a successful start in the guide business. For example, tour companies—the major employers of tour guides—know that good tour managers can influence passengers' decisions about taking repeat trips with the same company. So they are reluctant to take a chance on rookie guides.

Many tour guides sort of back into the field. They may be experts on certain subjects who start out as local guides to industrial plants or historical sites or who lead special agricultural tours or eco-tourism trips. These guides then move on to longer range, over-the-road tours. Licenses are required of guides in about five cities, but, for the most part, there are no formal requirements for becoming a tour guide.

As a practical matter, most guides are college graduates; many have graduate degrees. Indeed, some are former college professors—knowledgeable people used to lecturing who turn to this profession because of their love of travel. And while you could simply send your resume to tour companies, getting special training in tour guiding will give you a leg up in the field.

A number of community colleges and universities offer courses in tourism management and tour guiding. For the most part, these six- to eight-week courses are taught by practicing tour guides and managers who bring practical experience and their theoretical knowledge to students. One of the better programs in the country is at West Los Angeles College, where the faculty includes Marc Mancini, a veteran tour manager and author of several books on the field, including *Conducting Tours: A Practical Guide* (South-Western Publishing, 1991), which is considered the definitive tour-guiding textbook.

There are also proprietary trade schools that offer tour- guiding and managing programs. Many of them promote their ability to place graduates in jobs. Because these schools usually charge much more than public colleges, you should analyze their programs with care and a healthy skepticism. There are unscrupulous operators in this business who charge big bucks for superficial or even worse programs of instruction, with no money-back guarantees. The Professional Guides Association of America maintains a list of what it considers legitimate guide schools and training programs.

Some tour companies and destination management organizations, such as tourist bureaus, provide training to persons they hire for guide work. In many cases, in return for this training, you may be required to sign an agreement that you won't work for another company for a certain period of time. In the past, many guides learned their craft on- the-job with tour companies that simply gave them a chance to prove themselves in the field. However, as the travel industry becomes ever more sophisticated, such casual arrangements are disappearing. Since tour managers and guides are the front line employees in the group travel field, how well they perform may mean millions of dollars in sales gained—or lost—by tour companies.

If there are tour guides listed in your local phone directories, contact them and ask about how to get started in the business.

Your Future as a Tour Guide

Although more acutely attuned to the whims of the national and world economy than many businesses, the travel industry is expected to expand in the future as people's incomes rise, and they use their leisure time to visit places beyond their own communities. Group travel is a major segment of the travel business, and it is with this segment that tour guides and managers are associated. Employment prospects for guides should continue to expand in the years ahead.

The majority of professional guides—tour managers—are employed by group tour companies, such as Tauck, Maupintour, Globus Gateway, and American Express. The balance of the field is free-lancers, although some of these are more accurately small business operators who organize and guide their own specialty tours.

In many ways, tour guiding is akin to teaching, and guides who are able to work the maximum number of assignments through the year, which may consist of several touring seasons, can earn slightly less than the national average for teachers. Of course, free-lance guides don't have the job security and benefits of teachers. They get no health insurance, pension plan contributions, sick leave, paid vacation time, or unemployment compensation. And the work of a guide or tour manager isn't a typical nine-to-five job. Tour managers are on duty 24 hours a day for stretches of weeks at a time. A workweek of 85 hours is not unusual for a tour manager.

Of course, many free-lance guides like the fact that they can work as much or as little as they want to and that they can pick and choose assignments not necessarily for money, but for the enjoyment they figure they'll get from certain tours and particular itineraries. Also, gratuities are common in this field. While no guide can count on them, for popular guides, money from tips can be substantial over time.

Pay scales for tour guides vary by region. They are highest in the Northeast, Great Lakes, Mid-Atlantic and Southern regions; lowest in the Northwest, the West, and the Pacific Coast area. The range typically is $9.75 to $20 an hour. At those pay rates, and considering the seasonal nature of group travel, a successful free-lance tour guide-manager on the East Coast could expect to earn $17,000 to $20,000 a year. Tour managers employed by major tour companies will work more steadily and may enjoy valuable fringe benefits that free-lancers don't have. These employed tour managers and guides can earn up to $60,000 or $65,000 a year, including gratuities.

The more credentials a guide has, usually the higher the wage he or she will enjoy. In addition to college degrees and specialized courses, a valuable credential in the field is the Certified Professional Guide designation by the Professional Guides Association of America. Before a guide can even take the certification exam, 120 hours of field work is required. The certification must be renewed periodically through additional examinations.

For more information:

Professional Guides Association of America
2416 S. Eads Street
Arlington, VA 22202

International Association of Tour Managers
c/o Marion Gaston, North American Chairperson
80 N. Moore Street, #10G
New York, NY 10013

National Association of Interpretation
P.O. Box 1892
Fort Collins, CO 80522

International Guide Academy
Denver University
Foote Hall, #313
7150 Montview Boulevard
Denver, CO 80220

Miami-Dade Community College
Travel & Tourism Management Program
11380 N.W. 27th Avenue
Miami, FL 33167

West Los Angeles College
Department of Travel
4800 Freshman Drive
Culver City, CA 90230

Cruise Ship Crews

The ride may be smoother and the itinerary more glamorous if you assist passengers on a cruise ship, or on yacht charters, in the sunny climes of the Caribbean and other tropical resort areas.

Of course, there is a psychological downside to working on a cruiseship—all around you is beautiful sea, sky, and island landscapes, and happy, vacationing people, and you're working. Working on a cruise ship is not really like it appeared on "The Love Boat" TV series, with every bartender, waiter, and cabin steward having wonderful little tête-à-tête's with passengers. In fact, most of the ship's deck, cabin, and dining room workers are foreign nationals. Their quarters in the ship are spartan and skimpy and far removed from the spiffier cabins of the paying passengers. And crew meals are basic, the other side of the world from the culinary displays put on in the ship's dining rooms.

Cruise ships have a marine crew—as on merchant ships—of deck and engineering officers and seamen and oilers. The officers usually hail from the country on which the ship's cultural atmosphere is based—Norway, Greece, Italy, Britain.

Cruise ships also have what is called a hotel staff. These crew members include the purser (like a hotel front office manager), the cruise director (the social and public relations manager), managers of cabin and dining room services. They direct a large staff of deck and cabin stewards, dining room captains, waiters, bartenders, activity directors (of fitness classes, bingo games, lectures), and entertainers (who perform in clubroom shows and may double as activity directors during the day).

Because of the nature of their work, the cruise director's staff and activity directors have the most interaction with the passengers, but even they do not wine and dine with the paying customers. At dinner time and during the evening, they're usually stuck below decks with the rest of the ship's employees.

Hotel and marine crews usually do get shore time when the cruise ship is in port. Those ports are usually delightful. On the other hand, cruise ships are rarely in port for more than 12 hours.

But as a young nightclub lighting man on a Caribbean cruise ship says, "The pay's not great. The scene on the ship isn't idyllic. But there is the climate and having days off in some great places."

For cruise ship jobs, contact cruise lines directly. They are listed in the telephone Yellow Pages. Most are headquartered in Miami, New York, Los Angeles, and San Francisco.

CHAPTER TWO

The Transportation Industry

The Open Road: Trucking

The dream trip of many who long to travel is to motor across the land, observing the sweeping panorama of the landscape from highways and byways, free to stop wherever and whenever they fancy. "Now that's traveling!" they would say.

In a manner of speaking, you can take that trip—and get paid for it—as an over-the-road truck driver. From a perch six feet or so above the road, the driver of an 18-wheel tractor-trailer rig sees a panorama beyond the view of travelers in cars.

All of America is open to the exploration of long-haul truckers. During some part of its journey from producer to consumer, nearly everything is transported for some distance by trucks. Goods may also be shipped between terminals or warehouses in distant cities and countries by ship, plane, or train; but trucks usually do the hauling from factories to cargo terminals and from transfer points to stores and even homes.

Long-distance truck drivers are a familiar presence on the nation's interstates and major connecting highways. Their rigs—some with two or three tandem trailers—jockey for position in a lane that lets them maintain a steady speed. You can listen in, via CB radio, as truckers chat among themselves—and with cars sharing the highway—about the sights and scenes along the road.

The Daily Routine

Long-distance truck drivers are often away from home in their travels. On some long runs where pickups and deliveries are far apart, shipping companies use two drivers. One drives while the other sleeps in a berth compartment behind the cab of the truck. Sleeper runs may last for days—even weeks—with the truck usually stopping only for fuel, food, loading, and unloading.

On the other hand, some truckers have regular runs, transporting freight to the same cities on a regular basis. These trips can seem like just another day at the office. But with the schedule that most long-haul drivers have to maintain, there may not be much time for sight-seeing except from the windows of their cabs high above the highways.

Long-distance truck drivers spend most of their working time behind the wheel, but their job doesn't end when they step out of their cab at the end of a trip. When drivers reach their destination, or the end of their operating shift, they must complete reports about the trip and the condition of the truck. If there were any accidents, they have to file detailed reports about that.

Drivers also may be required to unload their cargo at their destination. For example, drivers of rigs that haul household furnishings around the country usually help with the loading and unloading at each end of their journey. They may hire several local day workers to help them. Some take helpers along on long runs.

Driving a tractor-trailer rig is a demanding job. There are a few more creature comforts in the cabs of the newest model than in older trucks—more comfortable seats, better ventilation, and improved cab design. However, driving for many hours at a stretch, unloading cargo, staying on the go in bad weather, dealing with heavy traffic, and traversing mountains can take a toll on drivers' nerves and physical stamina.

Drivers on long runs face boredom, loneliness, and fatigue. Although many drive mostly during the day, travel at night and on weekends and holidays is frequently necessary in order to avoid traffic delays and deliver the cargo on time and in good condition.

Work hours and other operating rules for interstate truckers are regulated by the U.S. Department of Transportation. For example, those rules stipulate that a long-distance driver cannot be on duty for more than 60 hours in any seven-day period and cannot drive more than 10 hours straight, which must be followed by at least eight consecutive hours off duty. Many drivers, particularly on long runs, work close to the maximum number of hours permitted.

Getting into the Business

Most truck drivers are employed by trucking companies or by manufacturing and distribution companies that have fleets of trucks to move the goods they make or sell. Fewer than one out of ten truck drivers is self-employed. Of these owner- operators, some operate independently, serving a variety of clients, while others lease their services and their trucks to trucking companies for assignment.

There are state and federal regulations setting qualifications and standards for truck drivers. All state regulations must meet federal standards; some state rules are more stringent than the federal regulations. At the very least, all truck drivers must have a driver's license issued by the state where they live, and most employers also prefer drivers with a good driving record. In most cases tractor-trailer drivers are required to obtain a special commercial driver's license (CDL) from the state where they live. All truckers who haul hazardous materials must have a CDL.

To obtain the CDL, you must pass a knowledge test and demonstrate that you can operate a commercial truck safely. All driving violations incurred by persons who hold commercial licenses are recorded permanently in a national data bank. So drivers whose commercial license is suspended or revoked in one state will find it difficult, if not impossible, to obtain a new one from another state.

Until they get their CDL, driver trainees must be accompanied by a driver with a CDL whenever they are behind the wheel of a truck.

Here are the Transportation Department's minimum qualifications for truck drivers engaged in interstate commerce: a driver must be at least 21 years old and pass a physical exam (employers usually pay for this) that shows the driver has good hearing, 20/40 vision with or without glasses, normal use of arms and legs, and normal blood pressure. In addition, drivers must pass a written exam on the Motor Carrier Safety Regulations of the Transportation Department.

Many trucking companies have higher standards. They may require drivers to be high school graduates and at least 25 years old, with three to five years experience as a truck driver. Many require annual physical exams for their drivers and may require drivers to submit to periodic drug screening as a condition of employment.

There are schools that train drivers, and they're not like those driver training courses for new motorists. Dealing with the multiple gears, the brakes, and the instrumentation of an 18-wheeler rig takes training and practice. Some truckers learn their occupation in the armed forces.

In addition to their truck driving skills and experience, owner-operators must have good business sense. It's a tough business. Many fail to make it pay off. Successful independent operators take courses in accounting, business, and similar subjects to be able to tackle all the paperwork involved in their business, and they often have a good knowledge of truck mechanics, which enables them to perform their own routine maintenance and do minor repairs on their rigs.

Employment Outlook

The U.S. Department of Labor predicts that jobs for truck drivers will increase at an average clip through the rest of this decade. Many trucking companies are reporting shortages of drivers. The exact number of openings at any time will vary because the amount of freight carried by trucks fluctuates with the economy. During economic slowdowns, some truck drivers may be laid off, and others may see their earnings drop with reduced work time or shipments. Owner- operators tend to be hit especially hard by slowdowns.

Truckers' earnings vary widely depending on weekly work hours, number of nights that must be spent on the road, and the type and size of the equipment they operate. Naturally, competition is stronger for the jobs with the best pay and working conditions.

As a rule, long-distance drivers are paid by the mile, and their rate-per-mile can vary widely from employer to employer. Earnings increase with total mileage driven, seniority with the company, and the size and type of truck they handle (most long-distance drivers operate tractor- trailers). Many companies also offer their drivers bonuses for good safety and on-time delivery records. Earnings typically range from as little as $20,000 to more than $50,000 a year. Most self-employed truck drivers are engaged primarily in long-distance hauling, and their earnings are commonly $20,000 to $25,000 a year after they deduct their living expenses and the costs associated with operating their trucks.

Many truck drivers are members of the International Brotherhood of Teamsters, Chauffeurs, Warehousemen and Helpers of America—the Teamsters for short.

For more information:

American Trucking Associations, Inc.
2200 Mill Road
Alexandria, VA 22314

The Teamsters Union
25 Louisiana Avenue, N.W.
Washington, DC 20001
(Or check your telephone directory for the local
union office.)

Tour Bus Drivers

If you decide that long distance truck driving isn't the kind of travel job you want because of the routine, not the driving, maybe tour bus driving will interest you. If it is the most glorious vistas and experiences you want to take in, this job can deliver.

The bus driver's job differs from the truck driver's work. For one thing, the itineraries of tour bus drivers link popular sightseeing, recreation, and entertainment destinations rather than city warehouse districts. The pace is usually more leisurely than that of truck drivers, although tour bus drivers may work nights, weekends, and holidays, just as truck drivers do.

Since they deal with human passengers, bus drivers must be able to get along well with people. The job requires them to be courteous. They need an even temperament and emotional stability because driving in heavy, fast-moving, and stop- and-go traffic—and dealing with passengers' needs and comfort—can be stressful.

However, because they sometimes carry the same passengers throughout a tour, which may last for a week or longer, tour bus drivers often share pleasant memories with their passengers. This chance to get to know the passengers can make the job more pleasant than driving a bus on a regular intercity schedule.

Getting into the Business

Like truck drivers, bus drivers must comply with state and U.S. Department of Transportation rules and requirements. They must obtain a Commercial Driver's License (CDL) just as truck drivers do, and bus drivers must meet health, age, and training standards comparable to those of truck drivers. Bus drivers should be able to handle some cargo, too. Handling passengers' suitcases, which must be stowed in luggage compartments underneath the passenger deck of the bus, is part of the job.

Tour bus drivers work for charter companies, which in turn are hired by tour companies to provide buses with drivers for specific tours. Some tour bus drivers may work directly for tour operators who run bus tours in major cities, tourist regions, or on routes that cross the country.

The work may be seasonal, since the major tourist travel time is May through September, although travel is becoming more year-round now, especially in long-weekend lengths. Of course, in major sunbelt areas, pleasure travel is a year-round business, and there may also be seasonal peaks in winter months.

During peak seasons and times, tour bus drivers may work the maximum number of hours allowed by Department of Transportation regulations.

Your Future as a Tour Bus Driver

Employment for tour bus drivers is very competitive. And the amount of available work can vary, as the travel business is highly sensitive to the whims of the economy, weather, and other factors.

Median earnings of tour bus drivers are comparable to those of intercity bus drivers and can depend on the number of miles they drive. Those who work about six months a year can earn about

$20,000, while senior drivers who work year-round might earn more than $40,000.

Drivers employed by tour operators and charter companies may enjoy health and life insurance and other fringe benefits. For those who are travel buffs, an additional benefit is being able to visit the country's prime tourist destinations—usually in ideal weather and with interesting people.

For more information:

The Teamsters Union
25 Louisiana Avenue, N.W.
Washington, DC 20001
(Or check your telephone directory for the local union office.)

National Tour Association
P.O. Box 3071
Lexington, KY 40596

Also ask your travel agent for the names of tour operators who offer bus tours in the United States. Two companies that do are Maupintour, Inc. of Lawrence, Kansas, and Tauck Tours, Inc. of Westport, Connecticut.

The Romance of Railroading

Train travel has declined in America over the years, but the romance of rail travel lingers. There is something about a train trip—the soothing click, clack of steel wheels on steel rails, scenes of wilderness in the hinterlands and of backdoor approaches to America's big cities, the niftiness of sleeping compartments, the pleasure of dining and bar cars.

The most popular passenger railroad routes in the United States are those that offer unparalleled scenic vistas—primarily those in the great western expanse of the country. Talk about romance, these trains have names—the California Zephyr, which runs from Chicago west through Denver and Salt Lake City to Oakland; the Empire Builder, which takes the northern route west to Seattle; and the Southwest Chief, which rolls south from Chicago through New Mexico and Arizona to the West Coast.

If you want a job that keeps you rolling over the rails, you can become a locomotive engineer or conductor on a freight train or an Amtrak passenger train. Or, you can go after one of the passenger service jobs available on Amtrak trains and become a bartender, cook, waiter or waitress in the dining and bar cars, or a host or hostess on long-distance sleeper trains.

The Life of a Railroader

Engineers are the top brass on train trips. Because they're in the driver's seat, they must be thoroughly knowledgeable about the rail system, signals and terminals along the route, and be constantly aware of the condition and makeup of their train. Trains react differently to acceleration, braking, and curves, depending on the number of cars, the ratio of empty to loaded cars, and the amount of slack in the train.

Engineers operate locomotives in rail yards, at train stations, and on the railroad between terminals. Most run diesel locomotives; a few run electric locomotives.

The engineer's chief aide is the conductor. On freight trains, conductors keep records of each car's contents and destination and make sure cars are added and removed at the right points along the route. On passenger trains, conductors also collect tickets and fares and assist passengers. At stops they signal engineers, telling them when to pull out of the station. On major Amtrack runs, there may be a conductor and several assistant conductors.

Before a train leaves its originating terminal, the railroad company's dispatcher gives the conductor and engineer instructions on the train's route, timetable, and cargo. The engineer and conductor discuss plans for the trip. Once underway, the conductor may receive additional information by radio—about track conditions ahead or the need to pull off the main track at the next available stop so another train can pass. The conductor then uses a two-way radio to contact the engineer and relay this and other instructions received from dispatchers and to remind the engineer of stops, reported track conditions, and the presence of other trains.

Since most trains operate 24 hours a day, many railroad employees often work nights, weekends, and holidays.

Getting into the Business

Most railroad workers begin as trainees for either engineer or brake operator jobs. Railroads prefer that applicants for these jobs have a high school education and mechanical aptitude and be in good physical condition—with good hearing, eyesight and color vision, eye-hand coordination, and manual dexterity. Applicants must pass a physical exam and tests that screen for drug use.

Most beginning engineers undergo six-month training programs that include classroom and on-the-job instruction. From that point, they work their way up to top engineer positions.

Conductor jobs usually are filled from the ranks of experienced brake operators who have passed tests covering signals, timetables, operating rules, and related subjects. Some companies require that candidates pass these tests within the first few years of employment in order to advance.

Your Future as a Railroader

Employment opportunities for railroad workers will be very limited through the rest of this decade and beyond. Overall employment in the industry continues to decline for several reasons. For one thing, demand is decreasing for railroad services because of price competition from airlines, bus, and truck lines. In addition, innovations such as larger, faster, more fuel efficient trains, and computerized rail yard systems, are making it possible for railroads to move freight more efficiently. Computers are used to keep track of freight cars, match empty cars with the closest loads, dispatch trains, and feed information and instructions to engineers. This increased reliance on computers means the railroads need fewer employees than in the past to move freight.

However, employment in the passenger train business seems to be holding its own. Amtrak continues to hire even though the freight side of the railroad business is static now.

If you manage to get a top job with a railroad company, salaries can be good. Annual earnings of locomotive engineers in passenger service average $54,600. For engineers in freight service, the average is $54,500. Conductors in passenger service average $47,200 a year; those in freight service average $50,800.

For more information:

Association of American Railroads
50 F Street, N.W.
Washington, DC 20001

Amtrak, National Passenger Railroad Corporation
Human Resources Department
60 Massachusetts Avenue, N.W.
Washington, DC 20002

Become an Airline Pilot

Airplane pilots are highly trained, skilled professionals. They can qualify to fly many kinds of fixed wing aircraft and helicopters. And they fly these craft on a variety of missions.

Most of us who travel are familiar with the role of passenger airplane pilots. You can see them going over their checklists in the cockpit or flight deck as you board a commercial jet airplane through the forward door. On some small commuter planes and corporate planes, you are in closer contact with the pilots; they may even supervise the seating of passengers and the stowing of their luggage in order to balance weight in the aircraft.

But there are lots of pilots whom we rarely see at work. For example, the pilots of cargo planes fly freight to destinations all over the world. Those who pilot the big jets for the overnight delivery services, like Federal Express, UPS, and Airborne, crisscross the United States on a regular schedule. Other pilots fly aircraft for aerial photographers or as test pilots for aircraft manufacturers or with forest fire-fighting crews. Some pilots work for the airlines as "examiners" or "check pilots." They periodically fly copilot to check on the proficiency of each pilot in the airline's employ.

Helicopter pilots are involved in police work, supplying off-shore oil platforms, land and sea rescue efforts, and major construction projects. They also transport passengers, often on sight-seeing tours.

About nine out of ten salaried civilian pilots work for the commercial airlines; others work as flight instructors at local airports; others, for corporations that use their own aircraft to fly company cargo and executives.

As they move up in seniority, airline pilots may opt for choice international routes or prime cross-country flights in the United States. This enables them to spend layovers of a day or two in far-flung cities of the world and premier tourist destinations. But this work style may not be rosy for all. Some veteran pilots complain about living out of a suitcase for much of their lives.

The Life of a Pilot

On most airplanes, two pilots usually make up the cockpit crew. The captain, generally the more experienced pilot, is in command and supervises all other crew members. The copilot, or first officer, assists in communicating with air traffic controllers, monitoring the aircraft instruments, and flying the plane.

Especially on larger airplanes on long international routes, there may be a third pilot on the flight deck—the flight engineer, or second officer, who assists the other pilots by monitoring and operating many of the on-board instruments and systems, making minor in-flight repairs, and watching for other aircraft. Since the latest technology can perform many flight tasks, in the future most aircraft will be flown by only two pilots. Current technology includes computerized controls and extensive video displays, which allow two pilots to get the aircraft from destination to destination fairly easily.

Because they have the help of large support staffs on the ground, airline pilots perform few nonflying duties; there are some, however. Before and after each flight, pilots do record-keeping paperwork for the airline and the Federal Aviation Administration (FAA), which licenses pilots to fly, sets standards for job requirements such as medical exams, and otherwise monitors pilots' careers.

Pilots who fly corporate aircraft may have many more nonflying duties in their job descriptions. They routinely supervise the fueling of their aircraft, check passengers aboard, load baggage onto the plane, and keep records on their flights and aircraft. In some cases, the pilot and copilot also attend to the needs of their executive passengers in flight, although on larger corporate planes, there may be at least one flight attendant to deal with the passengers. Corporate pilots might also find themselves scheduling flights, arranging for major maintenance, and even performing minor maintenance and repair work on their planes.

By federal law, airline pilots aren't allowed to fly more than 100 hours a month or more than 1,000 hours a year. Most airline pilots fly an average of 80 hours a month and work an additional 120 hours a month on nonflying duties.

Airlines operate flights at all hours of the day and night, so pilots' work schedules can be irregular. Based on seniority with the airline, pilots usually can choose particular flight routes and work patterns they prefer. Many of their flights require layovers away from home. The airline covers the cost of hotel accommodations, meals, ground transportation, and other layover expenses.

Pilots employed outside the airline industry often have irregular schedules. They may fly 30 hours one month and 90 the next. And because they frequently have many nonflying duties, they may have less time off than airline pilots. Except for corporate pilots, most pilots who work outside the airline industry don't encounter layovers in distant cities or even roam that far from home base in their flights. Their flying may be on a single short route, such as ferrying supplies and workers to offshore oil platforms or to construction sites.

Although flying does not require that much physical effort, the mental stress of being responsible for the safe flight of an airplane full of passengers, in all kinds of weather, can be taxing. The most stressful time for pilots is during takeoffs and landings, when they must be super alert and quick to react if something goes wrong. And, especially on international routes, pilots often suffer jet lag—disorientation and fatigue caused by many hours of flying through different time zones.

Getting into the Business

All pilots who are paid to transport passengers or cargo must have an FAA-issued commercial pilot's license with an instrument rating. Helicopter pilots must hold a commercial pilot's certificate with a helicopter rating.

Qualifying for these licenses takes some preparation. First, applicants must be at least 18 years old and have 250 hours or more of flying experience. They must pass a rigorous physical examination, have 20/20 vision, good hearing, and no physical handicaps that could impair their performance as a pilot. Applicants must also pass drug screening tests and a written test on the principles of safe flight, navigation techniques, and FAA regulations. Finally, they must demonstrate to FAA examiners their ability to pilot an airplane.

To be rated for instrument flying—in order to fly at night and in bad weather—pilot's license applicants must have a total of 105 hours of flight experience, including 40 hours flying by instruments. They must also pass a written exam on instrument flying procedures and regulations, and demonstrate their ability to fly by instruments.

Licensed pilots who join an airline, especially at entry level, usually must also pass written and in-flight examinations to earn a flight engineer's license. To become a captain, a pilot must have an airline transport pilot's license. Applicants for this license must be at least 23 years old and have a minimum of 1,500 hours of flight experience, including night and instrument flying.

All these licenses are valid as long as a pilot can pass the periodic physical examinations and tests of flying skills required by FAA and airline company regulations.

Flight Schools

So how do you begin? Where do you learn to fly? You do it in military or civilian flight schools. The FAA certifies about six hundred civilian flying schools, including some at colleges and universities that offer degree credit for pilot training. Novice pilots usually learn to fly on a small, single engine, fixed wing airplane. As they gain skill and experience, they move to training on twin engine craft and jets. Pilots trained in the military usually get substantial experience on jet aircraft and on helicopters, and this is highly valued by airlines and many businesses.

Most airlines require their pilots to have at least two years of college; they prefer four-year college graduates. In fact, most pilots entering the commercial field have a college degree.

Because pilots must be able to make quick and accurate decisions under pressure, airlines reject applicants who do not pass required psychological and aptitude tests. Yet, depending on the supply of capable pilots in the job market, airlines may loosen their educational requirements and even their 20/20 vision requirement, allowing vision corrected to 20/20, for instance.

Some airlines have also raised their maximum age limits for pilots in recent years to more than 50 years old.

New airline pilots usually start as flight engineers. When they join the airline, they receive several weeks of intensive training in flight simulators and classrooms before being assigned to a scheduled flight. Of course, once they are working for the airline, pilots regularly receive additional training to keep them abreast of technological advances such as wind-shear detection equipment and the like.

Career advancement for pilots generally is limited to other flying jobs. For example, a lot of would-be airline pilots start out as flight instructors for small flight schools, where they build up their flying hours while they earn money teaching. As they become more experienced, they occasionally fly charter planes or take on flying jobs with small air transport firms—like an air taxi company.

Then some of these pilots will advance to a corporate pilot's job or get a flight engineer's job with an airline. Once with an airline, advancement usually depends on the seniority provisions of pilots' union contracts. Typically, after two to seven years, flight engineers can advance, according to seniority, to copilot. Five to fifteen years after that, they can advance again and become a captain. A pilot who doesn't work for an airline may advance to chief pilot in charge of aircraft scheduling in a large corporate flight setup, or to manager of aircraft maintenance and flight procedures.

Your Future in the Sky

The job outlook for pilots should be favorable in the years ahead. Even though the number of airlines has decreased recently through mergers and buyouts, employment in the industry is expected to grow for a number of reasons. For example, before the end of this decade, job market analysts expect a wave of retirements by pilots who were hired in the late 1960s during the last major boom in the airline industry. Also, the military, which once provided the majority of pilots for the commercial airlines, has increased its benefits and financial incentives in an effort to retain more of its well-trained pilots. So the military is expected to be a diminishing source of new airline pilots.

College graduates who have experience piloting jet aircraft and who hold a commercial pilot's or flight engineer's license should have reasonably good job prospects in the airline industry. In fact, with an expected growth in airline passenger and cargo traffic through the rest of this decade (prompted by increases in population and income), government forecasters expect employment of pilots to grow much faster than average through the year 2000.

Airline pilots are highly paid. Starting salaries for flight engineers, the entry-level airline job for pilots, averaged about $18,000 in 1988. At the same time, the average salary for airline pilots was about $80,000 and for flight engineers, $42,000. Pay for airline captains averaged $107,000; for copilots, $65,000. Some senior captains of the largest aircraft can earn as much as $165,000 a year. Earnings depend on factors such as the type, size, and maximum speed of the plane and the number of hours and miles flown. Night and international flights sometimes bring a pilot extra pay.

Pilots who work outside the airline industry don't make as much. Average salaries for these pilots range from about $42,000 to $71,000, with the higher salaries usually going to pilots who fly jet aircraft.

Most airline pilots are members of the Air Line Pilots Association, International (AFL-CIO). Some flight engineers are members of the Flight Engineers' International Association (AFL-CIO).

For more information:

Future Aviation Professionals of America
4959 Massachusetts Boulevard
Atlanta, GA 30337

Air Line Pilots Association, International
1625 Massachusetts Avenue, N.W.
Washington, DC 20036

Flight Engineers' International Association
905 16th Street, N.W.
Washington, DC 20006
   For a list of FAA-approved flight schools, request a copy of
"List of Certificated Pilot Schools" from:

Superintendent of Documents
U.S. Government Printing Office
Washington, DC 20402

Flight Attendants

Is there any more glamorous figure in the lore of travel than the flight attendant? A perfectly groomed, trimly curvaceous, flaxen-haired girl with a perpetual smile, just waiting to bring you a drink or a meal or a pillow or magazine. That's the high-in-the-sky fantasy image.

In reality, flight attendants are women and men who serve aboard passenger planes to look after your safety and comfort during a flight. They generally are well-groomed, just as any workers who deal directly with the public should be, but they aren't all smiles, all blond, or all women. And they come in various shapes and sizes (although some airlines still are hard-nosed about weight standards for their passenger cabin crews).

Indeed, the routine of the flight attendant can be a decidedly unglamorous life at times, comparable to the job of a waitress or bartender.

Nevertheless, flight attendants do travel. Many of them make the most of it; particularly those who are young and carefree. It's a thrill to be able to hop a flight to the coast for a weekend or take your layovers in some of the most exciting cities in America.

The Daily Routine

At least an hour before each flight, attendants are briefed by the airplane's captain on such things as expected weather conditions for the flight and any particular passenger problems. The attendants check to see that the passenger cabin is in order, that supplies of food, beverages, blankets, and reading material are adequate and that first aid kits and other emergency equipment are aboard and in working order. As passengers board the plane, attendants greet them, check their tickets, and help them get settled—storing coats and carry-on luggage, finding a pillow.

Then it's time for the routine that is so familiar to anyone who has flown even a few times on scheduled airlines. Before takeoff the flight attendants line up in the aisle and instruct passengers in the use of emergency equipment—your seat cushion is a flotation device, lights along the floor lead to emergency exits, oxygen masks will drop down automatically if needed.

Then the attendants check to see that all passengers have their seat belts fastened and seat backs forward. Lead, or first, flight attendants oversee the work of the other attendants while performing most of the same duties themselves.

Assisting passengers in the rare event of an emergency is the most important function of attendants. This may range from reassuring nervous passengers during occasional bumpy encounters with strong turbulence to administering first aid to passengers who become ill to opening emergency exits and releasing evacuation chutes following an emergency landing. Flight attendants have been heroic in real emergencies and crashes. Some have lost their lives while trying to help passengers in these circumstances.

In the air, the attendants' routine is busy. They must deal with passengers' questions about the flight; distribute magazines and pillows; help make small children and elderly and handicapped persons comfortable; serve cocktails, soft drinks, and snacks; and, on some flights, heat and serve precooked meals. Of course, after snack or meal time, the attendants must collect all those rumpled napkins, empty cups, bottles, cans, plastic dinnerware, and trays.

And after the plane has landed and they have bid their passengers farewell, the flight attendants prepare reports on any medication given to passengers, lost and found articles, and the condition of cabin equipment. If this is an in-between stop, the flight attendants may have to tidy up the cabin before the next group of passengers boards the aircraft.

Since airlines operate around the clock, attendants may work at night and on holidays and weekends. They usually fly 75 to 85 hours a month and spend an additional 75 to 85 hours a month on the ground preparing planes for flight, writing reports following completed flights, and waiting for planes that arrive late.

Because of variations in scheduling and limitations on flying time, many attendants have 11 or 12 days, or more, off each month. They may spend the night away from their home base about one-third of this time. As they do for pilots, the airlines cover the cost of hotel accommodations, meals, ground transportation, and incidental expenses during layovers.

With their blocks of time off and the benefit of free flights on a standby basis for themselves and immediate family members, flight attendants can vacation in destinations they don't get to visit on the job.

If the free travel seems like a super fringe benefit, don't forget that the flight attendants earn it. Their work can be strenuous and trying. Short flights require speedy cabin service, especially if meals are served. A rough flight can make serving drinks and meals difficult—even dangerous. Attendants stand during much of the flight and must try to be pleasant and helpful no matter how tired they are or how demanding passengers may be.

Most flight attendants enjoy their jobs despite the hard work involved. Judy Schulte of Miami, Florida, spent her entire career as a flight attendant with Eastern Airlines. As a senior attendant, she opted for international and cross-country U.S. flights and traveled regularly to London, San Francisco, Las Vegas, New Orleans, and throughout the Caribbean.

Schulte has fond memories of some wonderful episodes in the air—like the time a live kangaroo in a suit (his handler was accompanying him to a promotional event) slipped out of his seat and bounded down the airplane aisle. And then there were the flights to Las Vegas—"For some reason, people would always ask, 'What time does the midnight show start?' I thought that was rather odd, so I would say eleven o'clock, and they would never bat an eye."

"I was there in the 1960s and 1970s, during the best years in the aviation industry," she recalls. "The airline was like family."

Getting into the Business

Most attendants work for commercial airlines, and most of them are stationed in major cities where the airlines have hubs or home bases. A small number of flight attendants work for large companies that operate their own corporate aircraft for business executives.

The airlines like to hire poised, tactful, and resourceful people who can deal comfortably with strangers. They must be in excellent health with good vision and the ability to speak clearly. Applicants usually must be at least 19 to 21 years old, but some airlines have higher minimum age requirements.

Applicants must be high school graduates; those who have completed at least several years of college or have experience in dealing with the public are preferred. Flight attendants for international airlines usually must be able to speak an appropriate foreign language fluently.

The major airlines usually require that newly hired flight attendants complete four to six weeks of intensive training in the airlines' own schools. Airlines that do not operate their own schools generally send their trainees to the school of a cooperating airline.

At these schools, the new attendants learn emergency procedures—such as evacuating passengers from an airplane, operating an oxygen system, and giving first aid. Attendants are taught flight regulations and duties, and company operations and policies. Trainees also receive instruction on personal grooming and weight control. Those who will work on international routes get additional training in passport and customs regulations and dealing with terrorism. After they graduate from the airline school, attendants must annually take 12 to 14 hours of training in emergency procedures and passenger relations.

When they first go from training school to the field, attendants are assigned to one of their airline's bases. The new attendants are placed on "reserve status," from which they are called to staff extra flights or fill in for attendants who are sick or on vacation. Reserve attendants "on duty" must be available on short notice.

Attendants usually remain on reserve status for at least a year; with some airlines, at some bases, it may take five years or longer to advance from reserve status. Once attendants move off the reserve list, they bid for regular base and flight assignments. Because assignment choices are based on seniority, usually only the most experienced attendants get their choice of base and flights.

Advancement takes longer today than in the past because experienced flight attendants are remaining on the job for more years than they used to. But eventually some long-time attendants transfer to positions as flight service instructors, customer service directors, recruiting representatives, or other administrative jobs.

Your Future as a Flight Attendant

Federal labor market experts project that employment of flight attendants will grow much faster than average through the year 2000. Growth in population and income is expected to fuel a rise in the number of airline passengers each year. Airlines will enlarge their capacity by increasing the number and size of their airplanes, and since FAA safety rules require one attendant for every 50 seats on board, more flight attendants will be needed.

On the other hand, you can expect keen competition for flight attendant jobs through the rest of this decade. The same government analysts figure the number of applicants will greatly exceed the number of job openings. Those with at least two years of college and experience in dealing with the public have the best chance of being hired.

Why the tough time getting a job if the number of jobs will be increasing so rapidly? It has to do with the image of the job. Despite the fact that airline travel today has become more like bus travel of old—with narrow, crowded seats, few amenities aside from peanuts and beverages, frequent and often lengthy connection stops at hub airports—the airline industry is still considered a "glamour" field by many new workers. After all, think of the travel involved, the chance to see more of America and the world than most people ever will. And the opportunity for free travel for airline employees and their families is an attractive fringe benefit.

Also, as more career-minded people enter this field, job turnover will decline. Even so, most job openings for flight attendants are expected to result from the need to replace attendants who retire or transfer to other occupations. Employment of flight attendants is also sensitive to cyclical swings in the economy. During recessions, when the demand for air travel declines, many flight attendants are put on part-time status or laid off. Until business picks up again for the airlines, few new attendants are hired.

Beginning flight attendants had median earnings of about $12,600 in 1988, according to the Association of Flight Attendants. The median for those with six years of flying experience is about $21,500 a year, and senior flight attendants earn as much as $38,000 or more a year. Flight attendants receive extra compensation for overtime work and for night and international flights. They are required to buy uniforms and wear them on the job. Uniform replacement items are usually paid for by the airlines, which also generally provide a small allowance to cover cleaning and upkeep.

Many flight attendants are dues-paying members of the Association of Flight Attendants, the Transport Workers Union of America, or other unions.

For more information:

Future Aviation Professionals of America
4959 Massachusetts Boulevard
Atlanta, GA 30337

Association of Flight Attendants
1625 Massachusetts Avenue, N.W.
Washington, DC 20036

Transport Workers Union of America
80 West End Avenue
New York, NY 10023

Other Airline Employees

Becoming a pilot or flight attendant isn't the only way for a travel buff to find a place in the airline industry. Most airlines offer their employees the opportunity to fly free, on standby status, or at reduced rates with reservations, anywhere on the airline's route. When they are off duty, reservation clerks, aircraft mechanics, baggage handlers, and other employees who work at airline sales and administrative offices are eligible for this fringe benefit—as are members of their immediate families.

CHAPTER THREE

Communications Careers

Travel Writers and Photographers

Among the occupations most directly tied to travel is that of the travel writer and photographer. Often one person plays both roles—writing travel stories and also taking the pictures to illustrate them. There is no question that travel writers travel.

And when they travel, travel writers often get the red carpet treatment—a bowl of fruit in the hotel room, an upgrade to business class on the plane, a personal guided tour of prime tourist sites, lavish meals in the best restaurants. Hotels, bed-and-breakfast inns, restaurants, cruise lines, theme parks, tour companies, airlines, and vacation destinations want travel writers to report good things about them. So when travel writers come calling, travel suppliers put on their best face.

Of course, the amount of special treatment travel writers receive usually depends on how much publicity they can offer in return. A visit by the travel writer whose articles appear in seven or eight newspapers in the heartland of America may not cause the heartbeats of hoteliers, chefs, and destination promoters to race. But when Robin Leach, host of the popular television travel shows, drops in, that's a different story. Travel suppliers want influential journalists to collect good impressions for the thousands of people who read their newspapers and watch their television shows.

To travel to the many destinations they write about, travel writers—especially the free-lancers—usually have to rely on some help from suppliers in the industry. If the writers had to pay top price for every hotel room, airline ticket, attraction pass, or cruise cabin, they would never get to travel to enough places to build the experience needed to advise readers and viewers about the best travel options. So, like travel agents, travel writers often go on familiarization trips that are sponsored by airlines, hotels, convention and visitors' bureaus, and other suppliers.

The Perfect Job?

Being a travel writer may sound like the perfect job for a travel buff, but there is a down side. First of all, not all travel writers get to travel to collect their information. Some travel writers and photographers are employed by newspapers, magazines, and guide book companies. When these writers travel, their company pays the bill, but this may not happen often. Many publishers stick to a strict budget, and their writers, editors, and photographers rarely get to travel; they get their travel information over the phone, by talking to people who really do travel.

And not every travel story requires travel. Travel writers need to know how the industry works. And that takes lots of research into airline fare structures, hotel operations, and the like. Travel writers don't write or broadcast reports only about tropical beaches, luxury hotels, and glamorous destinations. They must be able to tell their audiences how to get the best price deals on airline tickets and hotel rooms, how to protect themselves from pickpockets when on the road, where to find shopping bargains, how to avoid the crowds at popular destinations, and lots of other information on the mechanics of travel.

If a writer does need to travel to gather story material, he or she can often get special attention and discounts from travel suppliers. However, travel writers are frequently criticized for accepting such help to do their jobs. Those who object usually feel that special treatment and discounts will obligate the travel writer to give a favorable review to travel suppliers. In fact, the practice of offering bargains to travel writers is similar to giving free books or tickets to book or movie reviewers. And if writers and broadcasters are professionals with integrity, they'll tell their stories truthfully no matter how they managed to get where they needed to go to collect their story material.

Another drawback of being a travel writer is the pay. You probably won't ever get rich being a travel writer. Even those who are employed by newspapers and magazines—and those jobs are few—aren't in the top pay brackets. And for free-lance travel writers, the earning potential can be dismal. It's common for a writer to receive a paltry $10 or $15 for an article, with photographs, that fills an entire newspaper page. And the number of publications that purchase free-lance travel stories—even at these low rates—is limited.

Of course, for those who succeed, it can be a great career. The travel industry is a global enterprise and a major business everywhere in the world. The economies of whole countries, such as the Bahamas and Monaco, depend on tourism. Travel builds bridges of understanding among people throughout the world. Travel and tourism is an important subject and needs to be covered in the media. Travel writers are happy to do it, despite the potential drawbacks. As a wise travel writer would say, "It's tough work, but somebody's got to do it."

Public Relations

Whenever a new hotel manager is appointed, a brief story about the executive and his or her position is distributed to the media in the form of a press release. Before the start of each season, press releases about rates and attractions at resorts and tourist destinations go out to hundreds of travel writers and editors.

Cruise lines, tour companies, hotel chains, resorts, cities, and states all must keep the public aware of the delightful holiday and vacation opportunities they offer. These messages are continuously cranked out by cadres of public relations representatives who convey their information to the media in the hope that it will make the papers or the six o'clock news.

In order to write about the delights of the Doral Beach Club and Spa Resort in Miami Beach, a Royal Caribbean cruise, the beaches of the Bahamas, the fun and frivolity of Southern California, or the fjords of Alaska, public relations people must visit those destinations, check them out, and dig out facts and figures that they can pump into the stories they send out as press releases.

Public relations specialists work for every kind of business and institution. But those employed by companies in the travel and hospitality industry generally travel the most and to the glamorous locations.

Rich Steck, manager of media relations for Royal Caribbean Cruises in Miami, says of travel PR, "It's a lot of hard work, but it is also a fun job."

How and Where PR People Work

An organization's reputation, profitability—even its continued existence—may depend on how successfully it presents its goals, policies, plans, and products to the world. Public relations representatives devise and execute plans to mold the right image for the business or agency and to help promote its products and services.

Every kind of business and institution needs public relations people—businesses, government agencies, individuals, schools and universities, public interest groups, trade associations. And whatever the nature of the client organization, the public relations job usually requires some travel. PR people may go on the road to do field research on the client's properties, or to visit and build relationships with community and media representatives in areas where the client sells products and services.

Public relations involves not only telling an organization's story, but also understanding the attitudes and concerns of customers, employees, and the community at large and helping management formulate sound policies for dealing with those issues. Public relations representatives must deal with the press, community groups, government agencies and regulators, and political officials, as well as employees, suppliers, and customers.

In addition to plotting public relations strategy, PR reps dig up information, write news releases and speeches, accompany executives to media interviews and on public speaking engagements, and deal directly with inquiries from the press and public.

There are two kinds of public relations people—those who work directly for the business or institution they represent, such as a hotel chain or state tourism bureau, and those who work for independent PR agencies that have a client relationship with a number of different businesses. Often a business will utilize the services of both its own in-house PR reps and an outside agency. Most PR people work directly for institutions they represent; about 10 percent work for independent PR firms; another 10 percent are self-employed PR agents.

Independent public relations firms often specialize in certain kinds of clients. For example, some are well known for representing politicians and public figures like Hollywood stars and billionaires. Others specialize in handling the public images of specific kinds of businesses—banks and financial institutions, auto manufacturers, chemical companies, and travel industry clients such as hotels, resorts, cruise lines, tour operators.

PR reps with independent firms usually handle the accounts of specific clients; they are often called account executives.

Getting into the Business

Public relations has a long and colorful history. Its earliest days were marked by flackery, from which came the stereotype of the hustling, brassy publicity agent. As the field matured, though, its hard edges were smoothed. The profession became more polished; the techniques, more sophisticated; the operating rules, more reputable.

Today's PR people usually are college graduates. They must deal with top officials and managers of client companies and institutions, so a university background is necessary. Indeed, many colleges and universities offer degree programs in public relations, usually as part of their communications or journalism curriculum.

PR people as a rule are cool, sophisticated, smooth handlers of public pronouncements and media inquiries. Look at how well the U.S. armed forces PR officers (usually called public information officers when they work for the military, government, or public institutions) handled the often belligerent and irritating inquiries of the press during the Persian Gulf War.

As a PR person you don't have to be an expert on the business or product or service you are representing, but you should be able to quickly make yourself conversant on the basics of the subject. And you must know to whom you can refer the media for detailed, expert information. Of course, when you sit down to write a series of news releases, you can take enough time to do the research that will give your writing deeper authority.

The ability to research and communicate well through various media is a requirement for success in the PR field. Another key aspect of the work is being able to conceptualize the goals and objectives of an overall PR strategy and how the client's image and story should be communicated over time.

Qualifications for PR jobs include creativity, the ability to express your thoughts clearly and simply, good writing and public speaking skills, and a lot of drive and initiative. It also helps to have an outgoing personality, self-confidence, some understanding of human psychology, and an enthusiasm for motivating people.

Wise PR counsel is invaluable to companies, especially in emergency or extraordinary situations. When a series of deaths were caused in the United States by apparently poisoned patent medicine tablets, speedy, forthright, and savvy public relations efforts prevented customers from abandoning the product altogether. The manufacturer whose products were involved kept the public informed about everything it was doing to prevent further harm—removing all current stocks from the market, designing tamper-proof containers for future use, assisting the police in tracing the poisoner, and preventing similar acts.

Case Studies

Michelle Oaklan McFaul heads her own PR firm based in Mineola, New York. Before going into business for herself in 1991, she was the director of public relations for Loews Hotels, an international chain of upscale properties. Her independent agency now represents a number of other clients, mostly in the travel industry.

"In-house PR experience is invaluable," says McFaul, "because you learn so much more about the product you are representing."

From a job in sales and marketing with one hotel, McFaul worked her way to the top PR position in the chain. Her varied experience provided special insight. "I knew so many little anecdotes that I could pass on to the media to get their interest in the hotels, and I learned the difference between saying something at corporate headquarters and getting it done by the workers on the front lines in each hotel."

"When you represent hotels, you do get to travel to some glamourous locations," says McFaul, "but when you are there, you are 'on' every minute, because the management of that hotel expects you to inspect as many operations as possible and consult with all the managers and make so many contacts with the local press."

As an independent, McFaul misses being in on the day-to-day "scoop" that circulates in corporate corridors and being able to immediately sense changes in business priorities. But she will keep her firm small so she can offer her personal expertise and touch to every one of her clients.

Royal Caribbean Cruises' Rich Steck says the amount of travel he does in his work varies—some years it seems to him that he's not been on the road at all; other years, he remembers being continually on the go.

When he travels, Steck may escort press groups on his company's cruises, or supervise the filming of promotional films on a cruise (and work on the scripts each day as the filming proceeds). Steck recently traveled to the shipyard in France where Royal Caribbean's newest cruise ship is being built. There he gathered information he would circulate to the trade and consumer press.

Steck also travels to business and professional meetings and on occasional media tours—where he might escort the captain or cruise director of a Royal Caribbean ship "visiting 14 newspapers and radio stations in a couple of days. That's tough travel," says Steck.

He says travel companies whose in-house public relations operation is small may hire an outside PR agency to handle routine publicity work the staff just can't keep up with. But more commonly, outside agencies are hired for their specific expertise, such as producing a special event like the arrival in Miami of Royal Caribbean's *Sovereign of the Seas* on its maiden voyage. "That was one of the most spectacular events of this kind," says Steck.

Your Future in PR

Jobs for PR professionals are expected to grow at an average clip in the years ahead. With increasing business competition, even smaller companies and institutions are likely to need the services of PR people.

Salaries in the field are comparable with those in other business services occupations. The median earnings for PR people are about $28,790; the top 10 percent of practitioners earn more than $57,000, with superstars earning in the megabucks category.

Sources of more information:

Public Relations Society of America
33 Irving Place
New York, NY 10003

Society of American Travel Writers
1155 Connecticut Avenue, Suite 500
Washington, DC 20036

Association of Travel Marketing Executives
808 17th Street, N.W., #200
Washington, DC 20006

Publications on the field include:

The PR Reporter
P.O. Box 600
Exeter, NH 03833

Public Relations News
127 E. 8th Street
New York, NY 10024

Journalism

For many writers and photographers, reporters, correspondents, editors and electronic (radio, TV, video) journalists, travel is a way of life. They go wherever they must to pursue stories. Some accounts of how reporters tracked down the big story are as fantastic as the exploits of Indiana Jones in Stephen Spielberg's series of adventure movies. The open-mike reporting by CNN reporters of the bombing of Baghdad at the opening of the Gulf War seemed almost like a made-for-TV movie.

Reporters and correspondents for major news organizations—newspapers, magazines, television networks, and wire services—gather information and prepare stories that inform their audiences about what's happening in their home towns, their states, the nation, and in villages, cities, and countries around the world. They cover events, interview the people involved, and monitor the actions of public officials, corporate executives, special interest groups, and others who exercise power.

Some established journalists work on a free-lance basis, selling their work to publications, publishers, and other agencies. They sometimes are hired to complete specific assignments, such as writing about a new product or technique. Many writers and editors specialize in developing material for novels and non-fiction books and for magazines, trade journals, technical studies and reports, newsletters, and other publications and media productions.

Obviously, some journalists travel no farther than the other side of town to get their stories. But those who work for major periodicals and the TV network news organizations may roam the nation and the globe in their coverage. For some writers and photo journalists, the subject they cover is travel—how to travel, where to travel, how much it costs, when to go, which destinations are safest, most interesting, and the like.

A Writer's Life

In covering a story, journalists investigate leads and news tips, pour through documents, interview people, and make observations on the scene. They organize the material they've gathered, decide on a focus or emphasis, and write their stories to meet the deadlines of their papers or wire services, or radio or TV stations. Many of them write on portable laptop computers and send their word processed stories by phone modem to their newspaper's or magazine's computer system.

Video journalists usually work in tandem with a camera and sound crew on the scene of their story. They often compose their story on the spot and report it live from the scene via microwave and satellite transmitting facilities. Or back in the studio, they work with a video editor to prepare a taped report with pictures and narration. In the TV field, producers usually are the equivalent of newspaper reporters; they research and pull together information for live or taped video programs and reports. The "talent"—a station personality or news "anchor"—may actually appear on camera to deliver the producer's report.

Large newspapers and broadcasting stations and networks assign reporters to specific "beats"—either geographic locations, areas of interest, or specialized fields. A journalist's beat might be police, courts, military, the White House, Congress, state legislatures, health, politics, foreign affairs, sports, fashion, art, education, or business. Many news and information organizations station correspondents in major U.S. cities and in foreign countries to cover events occurring in these locations.

Reporters on small newspapers may cover all aspects of the local scene and also take photos, write headlines, lay out pages, edit wire service copy, and write editorials. On some small weeklies, they may even have to sell subscriptions, solicit advertisements, and perform general office work.

There are all kinds of specialists within the world of journalism. In addition to reporters, TV producers, and editors, there are TV anchors, who may rarely leave the studio except for publicity appearances. Anchors read the newswriters' reports on the afternoon and evening newscasts.

Columnists analyze news and write commentaries based on personal knowledge, experience, and opinion. The TV version of the columnist is the participant in the news discussion-group show.

Editorial writers produce comments they hope will stimulate or mold public opinion.

Editors do some writing and, almost always, do much rewriting and editing of the work of reporters and writers. Often their primary duties are to plan the contents of books, magazines, newspapers, and news broadcasts and to supervise their preparation. Editors decide what will appeal to readers and viewers; they assign topics and events for reporters to cover.

Working conditions for writers and editors vary depending on where they work and what kind of material they produce. Some work in comfortable, private offices; others work in noisy rooms filled with the sound of keyboards and computer printers and the voices of other writers on the phones tracking down information. When reporting from the scene, radio and television reporters often have to work despite the distraction of curious onlookers, police, and other emergency workers. Of course, assignments to cover wars, political uprisings, fires, floods, and such can be downright dangerous.

Journalists' working hours vary. They typically work a 40- hour week, but their schedules can be irregular. For example, reporters on morning papers usually work from late afternoon until midnight; those on afternoon or evening papers work from early morning to early or midafternoon. Radio and television reporters generally work a day or evening shift. Magazine reporters, writers, and editors generally work during the day, although even they may have to work odd hours to meet a deadline or follow late-breaking developments in major stories. Foreign correspondents may work late at night to meet schedules in different time zones back home.

Jobs with major book publishers, magazines, broadcasting companies, advertising and public relations firms, and the federal government tend to be concentrated in major cities—New York, Chicago, Los Angeles, Boston, Philadelphia, San Francisco, Washington, D.C.. Writing and editing positions with newspapers, corporations, and religious, business, technical, and trade union magazines or journals are found throughout the country.

The pace of journalists' work can be hectic. They usually are under great pressure to get the story and write it in time to make a newspaper or magazine or radio or TV deadline. There are always deadlines.

The search for firsthand information often requires travel. A journalist may visit diverse workplaces, from factories and mines to offices and laboratories, theaters and ballparks. Sports writers follow the teams they report on. They may accompany the players on planes and buses in their journeys to far-flung stadiums and playing fields.

Of course, journalists don't always have to travel to get their information. The job involves a lot of telephone interviewing and library research. Even when writing about travel, writers can sometimes finish their stories without needing to travel and gather firsthand information.

Getting into the Business

About seven out of ten reporters and correspondents work for newspapers, either large city dailies or suburban and small town dailies or weeklies. Almost two in ten work in radio and television broadcasting; others work for magazines and wire services. Of salaried writers and editors, about 40 percent work for newspapers, magazines, and book publishers. A substantial number work on journals and newsletters published by business and nonprofit organizations, such as professional and trade associations, labor unions, and religious organizations. Some work in radio and television and for government agencies. Others write and edit material for advertising agencies, public relations firms, and large corporations.

Thousands of writers and photographers work as free-lancers—selling their articles, books, pictures, and scripts wherever they can. In most cases, their markets are major newspapers and magazines and publishers. It's not a very reliable way to make a living, and most free-lancers support themselves primarily with income from other sources.

Most employers prefer to hire college graduates with a degree in journalism, English, or communications. They may also look for job candidates with experience on school newspapers or broadcasting stations or as interns with news organizations. For jobs at some major newspapers and broadcasting stations, an educational background in subjects related to specific beats such as economics, political science, or business can help you get the job. Fluency in a foreign language might be necessary for assignment to an overseas bureau.

All writers and editors must be able to express ideas clearly and logically. Creativity, intellectual curiosity (a "nose for news"), a broad range of knowledge, initiative, and persistence are valuable characteristics. You'll also need the ability to concentrate amid confusion and produce under pressure. Other assets are poise and resourcefulness, a good memory, physical stamina, and emotional stability—to deal with pressing deadlines, irregular hours, and sometimes dangerous assignments. Journalists who work in unfamiliar places must be adaptable and feel at ease with a variety of people.

It should go without saying that reporters and writers need good typing/word-processing skills. And a knowledge of photography is often a plus. Many entry-level positions are combination reporter–camera operator or reporter–photographer jobs. Those who pursue electronic journalism should feel at ease on camera or in front of a microphone. Because reporting and writing require research, you also should be familiar with various research techniques.

Most beginners start out with small publications or stations. To join a larger paper or station usually requires several years of reporting experience. Only a few make it to the major city papers and stations, the broadcast networks, and national magazines.

In small operations, beginning writers and editors may do a little bit of everything—from reporting and writing to editing and laying out pages of stories and photographs. Advancement may come only by moving to a bigger paper or station. In larger organizations, jobs usually are structured more formally. Beginners generally do research, fact checking, and copyediting. Eventually they take on full-scale writing or editing duties. Advancement comes as they are assigned more important articles to write or edit.

The job of journalist will afford you an opportunity for self-expression, but more important is your ability to present facts as objectively and succinctly as possible. Accuracy also is vital because, among other things, untrue or libelous statements can lead to costly lawsuits.

Some experienced reporters become correspondents, roving editors and writers, announcers, or public relations specialists. Others become managing editors or electronic media program managers.

Your Future as a Writer

Employment of reporters and correspondents should grow at an average clip through the rest of the decade, primarily as a result of anticipated growth in the number of small town and suburban daily and weekly newspapers. Also, some growth is expected in radio and TV stations. But little or no growth is expected among big city dailies.

The need to replace reporters who leave the field will create most job openings. There is a lot of turnover in this occupation; many find the work and life-style too stressful and hectic, and they transfer to other occupations where their skills are valuable, especially public relations and advertising work.

Competition can be intense for reporting jobs on major metropolitan newspapers and broadcast stations and on national magazines. Most beginning journalists start out with papers and stations in suburban areas and small towns. To advance their careers from positions on small publications, reporters may become editors when openings occur or transfer to jobs on larger publications. Talented writers who can handle highly specialized scientific or technical subjects will be at an advantage in the job market.

Actually, employment of salaried writers and editors by newspapers, periodicals, book publishers, and nonprofit organizations should grow faster than average—largely due to the growing demand anticipated for publications in general. Growth of advertising and public relations agencies should also be a source of new jobs for writers. As with reporters and correspondents, job openings for writers and editors will also occur as experienced workers transfer to other fields or leave the labor force through death and retirement. Competition for these jobs, too, will continue to be stiff, primarily because so many people are attracted to the field.

Demand for technical writers is expected to increase because of the continuing expansion of scientific and technical information and the need to communicate it. The competition for technical writing jobs may not be as keen as for other areas of the writing business because of the more limited number of writers who can, and want to, work with technical material.

Pessimists advise persons considering a career in writing and editing to keep their options open. Academic preparation in another field may prove useful—either to qualify for a specialty area writing job or for another occupation.

Starting salaries for reporters working for daily newspapers under Newspaper Guild contracts range from about $13,000 to about $26,000 a year. For experienced reporters the minimums range from about $20,800 to $41,600. Senior editors on large circulation newspapers and magazines average over $60,000 per year.

Annual salaries of radio reporters range from about $12,000 at the smallest stations to about $30,000 at large city stations. TV reporters earn from about $15,000 in small market stations to about $67,400 in the largest markets.

Salaries for beginning writers and editorial assistants generally range from $18,000 to $26,600 annually. Experienced writers and researchers generally earn between $20,800 and $37,900 a year, depending on their qualifications and the size of the publications for which they work. For experienced editors, salaries typically range from $22,200 to $39,800; for supervisory editors, $32,600 to $49,400.

Salaries for technical writers range from $19,800 to $46,300. Writers and editors employed by the federal government earn an average of better than $31,000 a year.

Starting salaries for copy editors on daily papers can be quite low. That's why many writers and editors supplement their salary income by doing free-lance work.

For more information:

American Newspaper Publishers Association Foundation
The Newspaper Center
Box 17407
Dulles International Airport
Washington, DC 20041

American Society of Magazine Editors
575 Lexington Avenue
New York, NY 10022

Association for Education in Journalism and
    Mass Communication
University of South Carolina
College of Journalism
1621 College Street
Columbia, SC 29208

The Dow Jones Newspaper Fund
P.O. Box 300
Princeton, NY 08540

National Newspaper Association
1627 K Street, N.W., Suite 400
Washington, DC 20006
(publishes a pamphlet: "A Career in Newspapers")

The Newspaper Guild
Research and Information Department
8611 2nd Street, N.W.
Silver Spring, MD 20910

Society of American Travel Writers
1155 Connecticut Avenue, Suite 500
Washington, DC 20036

Society of Technical Communication, Inc.
815 15th Street, N.W., Suite 516
Washington, DC 20005

Publication:

Editor & Publisher International Year Book
Editor & Publisher
11 West 19th Street
New York, NY 10011
(This book can be found in most libraries.)

CHAPTER FOUR

Business and Government

Top Executives

No matter what your field, when you reach the top echelons of the business world, odds are great that your job will require you to travel—to visit your lieutenants in the field, inspect far-flung offices and plants, attend conferences, meet with major clients in locations around the world. Chief executives of major corporations may even fly in their own corporate jets.

At this level of the American work force, when you work hard, you play hard as well. A business trip that takes you across the country might be extended for a day or two, so you can play a little golf and unwind at a resort. Also, when captains of industry travel to conferences and meetings, their wives may accompany them.

What are the jobs that offer these perks? These are the positions of corporate chairperson, president, and vice presidents—who usually include a company's chief executive officer, chief operating officer, and chief financial officer—as well as top executives and managers of major plants, stores, regional and branch offices. Many top-tier lawyers, physicians, college presidents, real estate developers, and financial dealers also operate in this style.

As you'll see later in this chapter, some public officials may enjoy travel and other aspects of the top executive life-style. But unlike private sector executives, the working routines of government chiefs are subject to wide public scrutiny—through the media. And they can risk scandal if they indulge in an executive work style that is too fancy for the taxpayers to tolerate.

The *Washington Post*, *New York Times*, CBS's "60 Minutes," and other media watchdogs relish stories of bureaucrats who use government planes to travel to ski resorts and summer homes, attend lavish soirees hosted by lobbyists, take study trips to locations like Paris, Rome, the Bahamas, and attend conferences at resorts with golf courses, saunas, and sandy beaches.

The Daily Routine

In jobs at the top of the management hierarchy, you formulate policy and direct the operations of companies and government agencies. An organization's chief executive collaborates with the board of directors and other top executives to move the entity on its course. In a large corporation, a busy CEO meets frequently with top executives of other corporations, government agencies, bankers, lawyers, and major customers. The work of running the operation is delegated to scores—even hundreds—of managers. How many top execs there are depends on the size and scope of the enterprise, of course.

Some multimillion-dollar organizations are run by a tightly knit group of several dozen managers in a single location. Other corporations are mammoth—with hundreds of top executives occupying a skyscraper and hundreds more in scores of plants and branch offices around the country or around the world.

Top executives may be provided with spacious offices and numerous perquisites, such as private dining rooms, cars, club memberships, and liberal expense accounts. These are meant to facilitate executives' meetings and negotiations with other corporate chiefs, customers, government regulators, and ministers of foreign countries where the company has assets.

Of course, it's not all three-hour lunches and limo rides at the top. Long work days, including evenings and weekends, are the rule for most captains of industry. You might say they are always on call. Business discussions may occupy most of an executive's time at social engagements, on the golf course, while fishing on an important client's yacht. It's hard to tell where business life ends and private life begins for many industry chiefs.

In large corporations, job transfers between headquarters and the company's far-flung network of plants, offices, and subsidiaries are common. To climb to a top post in a major corporation, you might move your household to a new city five or six times over 20 years. Spouses and children have to adjust to this mobile life.

Managers work under often intense pressure to attain goals in production and sales, for instance. You can find yourself in situations in which you have limited influence—for example, meeting new requirements of government regulations, or dealing with unexpected pressures from competitors or public interest groups, or facing natural or financial catastrophes.

Travel is practically a given in the corporate world. Airlines created frequent flyer clubs—with all their rewards, proffered creature comforts, and other enticements—to capture their share of the travel time—and dollars—of this peripatetic group of workers who keep airplane seats filled throughout each workweek. Some executives enjoy frequent travel; others view it as a chore.

Corporate executives and government bureaucrats travel between regional and local offices in the United States and overseas. In the global economy that exists today, American managers conduct business around the world. To keep up with developments in their fields and network with their peers, executives regularly attend meetings and conferences in locations far from the home office.

Because work keeps them on the road so frequently, many of those conferences are held at properties where the management men and women can relax together after their work sessions—at receptions and dinners, golf and tennis matches, and the like. Many top executives are reimbursed for the traveling expenses of their accompanying spouse, since the wives and husbands of corporate managers assist them in corporate socializing.

Getting into the Management Stratosphere

The educational background of top executives varies as widely as the nature of their diverse responsibilities. Most of them have a college degree. Graduate and professional degrees are common in this group. The Master of Business Administration (MBA) and Master of Public Administration (MPA) remain in vogue.

On the other hand, the degree may not be related to the executive's present field of work. And many top execs got to their lofty positions by dint of their own personal genius or hard work and have little formal schooling of any kind.

But if you want to plot out a course for becoming a world-traveling corporate executive, your odds will be greatest if you have an appropriate college degree—such as business administration, public services or education administration, economics, finance, statistics, psychology, urban studies, and the like. A degree will help you get into position to climb the corporate management ladder.

However, making the climb usually calls for much more than simply an appropriate degree. Most top executive positions are filled by promoting experienced lower-level managers who display the leadership, self-confidence, motivation, decisiveness, personality, and corporate loyalty required in the executive suites.

In small firms, where the number of positions is limited, advancement to the upper strata of management can be excruciatingly slow. In giant firms, promotions may come quicker, as there are many more intermediate levels where you can prepare for a top management position. Another advantage in larger firms is that there often are company training programs that broaden your knowledge of company policy and operations in a timely fashion and thereby accelerate your passage through the hierarchy.

There is more than one path to the top. Instead of joining a company as an entry-level employee and working your way up the ladder there, you might climb faster by hopping from company to company, or by starting your own firm after learning what you need to know at the big corporation.

As a rule, to become a top-tier manager, you should have highly developed personal skills, an analytical mind able to quickly assess large amounts of information, the ability to consider and evaluate the interrelationship of numerous factors and select a successful course of action. You should also have sound intuitive judgment and be able to communicate clearly and persuasively, both orally and in writing.

Your Future in Top Management

Employment of top managers and executives should increase at an average pace through the end of the decade as businesses grow in number, size, and complexity. However, as competition intensifies internationally, and many firms improve their operating efficiency by expanding individual managers' responsibilities, that will moderate employment growth in the top corporate ranks.

Executive employment growth will vary by industry, too. For example, most services industries will continue to expand rapidly. And very rapid employment growth is expected in firms that supply management, consulting, public relations, personnel and other business services because more firms will find it cost-efficient to contract out for these services. Executive employment should also grow rapidly in accounting, bookkeeping, and auditing services firms and in industries concerned with health and welfare, such as outpatient clinics and agencies offering individual and family social services.

On the other hand, employment of managers and top executives is expected to increase more slowly in the educational services industry, matching the modest growth of the school- age population. And there may be little or no growth—possibly even a decline in employment—in some manufacturing industries where business is being lost to foreign plants.

Salary levels of top executives vary substantially depending on many variables—the exec's managerial responsibility, length of service, particular specialty and experience, and the type, size, and location of the firm. The estimated median annual salary of general managers and top executives was about $38,700 in 1988. But many earned well over $52,000.

Most salaried executives in the private sector receive additional compensation in the form of bonuses, stock awards, and cash-equivalent fringe benefits such as company- paid insurance premiums, physical examinations, paid country club memberships, use of company cars, and the usual paid vacation time, sick leave, and pensions.

Salaries also vary substantially by industry and geographic location. For example, salaries in manufacturing and finance are generally higher than those for corresponding executive positions in state and local government. And salaries in large metropolitan areas are normally higher than those in small cities and towns. Some surveys of executive salaries reveal that a top manager in a very large corporation can earn 10 times as much as a counterpart in a small firm.

CEOs—chief executive officers—are the most highly paid top-level managers. Recent surveys of major corporations show that more than 150 U.S. CEOs receive base salaries of a million dollars or more, plus additional compensation, such as fringe benefits and company stock, equivalent on the average to nearly half of their base salary. With that kind of money, you can travel anywhere in the world without undue strain on the pocketbook.

For more information:

American Management Association
Management Information Service
135 W. 50th Street
New York, NY 10020

National Management Association
2210 Arbor Boulevard
Dayton, OH 45439

Politics

Another way to travel in your work is to get elected or appointed to public office at the state or national level. The president of the United States has probably the largest executive jet in the world, and when he travels, they really do roll out a red carpet.

Governors, lieutenant governors, members of the U.S. Congress, and chiefs of top-level state and federal bureaus and departments routinely travel on business. Their travel patterns are similar to those of their corporate cousins in the private sector.

Government executives and elected officials make study trips, often with spouses and staff associates, to exotic and workaday destinations around the world—to attend conferences, solicit business investment or tourism from other states and countries, look at how U.S. aid is being spent in foreign lands, or meet with their compatriots in other governments. As mentioned earlier, such trips sometimes cause negative publicity for politicians. Occasionally, media critics describe some of these trips as extravagant and unnecessary junkets, on which the public servants are wining and dining at taxpayer expense.

Legislators receive allowances for travel from Washington, or their state capitols, to their home districts during the year. Many

U.S. senators and representatives also travel around the country for speaking engagements where their travel expenses are covered by the host groups, and they might receive an honorarium as well.

Getting yourself into such a position can be a long and arduous process of working with local political organizations for a chance to be nominated to run for office or be appointed to one. Politicians must raise lots of money to pay for election campaigns, which are risky. There are as many losers as winners, and both have to pump dollars into their campaigns.

Even the path to a top appointive government job—like head of a department or agency—can require years of volunteer work and networking or being well connected to a politician who is in a position to make the appointments you covet.

Preparing for a shot at being a top government executive is similar to preparing for top jobs in the corporate world. But the road to the top in government is less structured. It can be traversed more quickly (if your candidate wins, you can gain an appointed job overnight), but it is usually more chancy than advancement in the world of commerce.

Become a Meeting Planner

Meeting planners plan business meetings. That might sound simple to you—until you recognize that these meetings aren't just for two people conversing across a desk, or even a dozen people sitting at a conference table. The meetings in question are usually major affairs involving hundreds to thousands of people at sites around the world. They are conventions, expositions, and trade shows.

Indeed, planning and running such meetings is a gigantic industry. Just think about all the businesses involved in putting on a national or international convention—hotels and a convention center, of course, and caterers, restaurants, printers of posters and program books, phone companies to rig up communication systems, bus and cab lines to haul delegates around, security services to keep them safe, musicians and other entertainers, audiovisual firms that put together slide shows, airlines that serve the convention city, and more. A major convention may draw eight to ten thousand or more people. And it can pump hundreds of thousands of dollars into the economy of a city. It's been estimated that $35 billion a year is spent in the United States on meetings.

The people who organize these big operations are professional meeting planners. It's a relatively new profession, of course, but one that is solidly established in the business world today.

Meeting planners perform a variety of functions in mounting conferences, from preparing a budget for the operation and selecting the site and facilities for the meeting to creating the meeting program and actually running the meeting at the site.

They must travel to dozens of cities to check out convention facilities and negotiate group rates for hotel accommodations, meals, and air and ground transportation for thousands of delegates who will attend the meetings. Planners must set up a system for registering delegates in advance and booking their room reservations. They must plan food and beverage functions, book entertainment for convention events, coordinate the production of printed and audiovisual materials, set up meeting and conference rooms, engage speakers, and organize a trade show with hundreds of exhibitors.

How and Where They Work

Most U.S. associations and large corporations have a meeting planner or staff of planners. Many planners back into the profession; they become experts at planning meetings because they're required to arrange meetings for their company, even though they weren't trained to do so. Their primary duties may have been in public relations or marketing or in other administrative areas.

But as meetings become a more important and costly function for businesses, the people assigned to manage them become increasingly professional at this job. These days, meeting planners tend to be well-educated people who are making a career of this corporate function. Typically they have college degrees, a working knowledge of the travel industry, and effective written and verbal communication skills. Meeting planners must interact well with all types of people and make important decisions even under pressure.

By far the greatest number of meeting planners are employed by corporations and by trade and professional associations. But there are some independent planners who work as consultants to companies that need meetings planned, but do not have people within their organizations who can handle that duty.

Getting into the Business

An effective meeting planner must know how to function as a businessperson first and then specifically as a meeting planner. The background usually required of a meeting planner includes a four-year college degree, preferably in business administration, marketing, management, or communication. Some planners come from college programs in hotel/motel management.

Beyond college, professional development programs and advanced training are available to planners through associations and other organizations in the field.

Often, getting your first job as a meeting planner is tough without experience. But how do you get experience, if you can't get the job? Many planners do it by working in convention sales for a hotel, where hosting business meetings is a major source of revenue. Others work as an intern or assistant to a planner. Some gain experience by volunteering to plan activities such as office parties, community organization events, and church outings. Even if you don't get paid for your work, the experience is valid.

Landing a job as a professional meeting planner is very competitive. To be successful at it, you need a strategy for scouting out potential employers, then finding effective ways to make your pitch to them. Of course, you should review help-wanted ads in publications in the field, in your local newspapers, and in almost any kind of trade journal (since nearly every trade association has meetings and a meeting planner).

Meeting Planners International, the industry's leading educational and networking organization, promotes the professional growth of meeting planners through its educational programs and its own meetings—nationally and in its 43 chapters around the world. Planners with an adequate amount of working experience in the field who complete certain professional requirements can earn the designation of Certified Meeting Professional, a credential that greatly enhances their employability.

Your Future as a Meeting Planner

Professional meeting planners will find their field growing in numbers of jobs in the years ahead. Americans, and people of other countries, are meeting more often at events that require professional planning and operation. With the growing emphasis on adult and continuing education and the need for networking and exchanging information in all fields of work, meetings play a key role in giving attendees a competitive edge in their careers. This trend promotes demand for qualified meeting planners.

The positions meeting planners hold in companies and associations vary. Most are in the middle management sphere, but a good number work in top management positions. Of course, salaries range accordingly. Typically, salaries for entry-level planners average in the mid- to upper-teens. Salaries for more experienced planners range into the $30,000 level and beyond.

For more information:

Meeting Planners International
1950 Stemmons Freeway
Dallas, TX 75207

Sales

Once the image of the traveling salesman was of a huckster toting a sample case full of kitchen utensils door to door in residential neighborhoods.

Today's traveling salespeople may circle the world in pursuit of million dollar contracts for power plants, high-tech electronics, and custom-designed computer systems. Obviously, all salespeople aren't globe-trotters, but most who work for major companies find travel is a fact of life. And as markets become more global, national boundaries fall before the sales corps.

Think of the thousands of products that are sold and bought each day—from bags of potato chips, romance novels, and sneakers to precision computer chips, giant construction equipment, and thousands of other products. The makers of the products employ sales representatives to market their products to manufacturers, wholesalers and retail stores, government agencies, and other institutions. They deal with buyers and purchasing agents.

Depending on where they work, these sales reps have different job titles. Most are referred to as manufacturer's, or wholesale, reps; those who sell technical products may be called industrial sales reps or engineers.

Manufacturers', wholesale, and industrial sales reps may be employees of the firms whose goods and services they sell, or they may be self-employed agents who contract their services to various companies. Often contract reps specialize in selling particular lines of products and services. Some self-employed reps build sales companies that employ scores of salespeople who service client manufacturers.

The Daily Routine

Manufacturers' reps spend much of their time traveling to the offices and plants of prospective buyers. During sales calls, they show samples, pictures, and catalogs of items their company stocks. They may discuss the customer's needs, then suggest how their company's merchandise can meet those needs.

Sales reps must know about prices, availability, specifications, and performance of the products they sell and how they can save money and improve productivity for the buyers. Because of the vast number of manufacturers and wholesalers selling similar products and services, they might emphasize the prompt delivery and dependable follow-up services offered by their company.

The sales reps usually are the people who must resolve any problems or complaints with the merchandise and services they sell.

Often these manufacturers' reps sell products and services that must be custom designed for the buyers, who are usually large corporations. For example, selling computers to a company may mean designing a unique system of hardware, software, and peripheral equipment to handle a particular company's type of business. Or a machine product may have to be designed or modified to work in a certain way within a specific amount of space.

That's why manufacturers' sales reps often must know much more about the field in which their products are used than do salespeople for consumer goods and less sophisticated merchandise. Industrial sales engineers, for instance, usually are qualified engineers as well as sales agents. They typically sell products whose installation and optimal use require a great deal of technical expertise and support—industrial robots, mainframe computers, manufacturing and assembly-line machinery.

In addition to providing information on their manufacturers' products, most reps help prospective buyers with technical problems and questions. For example, they might recommend improved materials and machinery for a customer's manufacturing process, draw up plans for how the proposed machinery would be used, and project cost savings that could result from the purchase of their equipment.

Such a sale isn't short and sweet. It may take weeks, or months. It involves a process of negotiation. Salespeople present their proposals; the customer's managers react with questions or suggested modifications in the deal. The price is rarely fixed; it will depend on so many variables in the deal. The sales reps may work with engineers in their own companies, who adapt products to the customer's special needs. After the deal is done, the sales rep may make frequent follow-up visits to ensure that the equipment is functioning properly and may even get involved in training the customer's employees to operate and maintain the new equipment.

Of course, independent manufacturers' reps must also manage their own businesses; they often have one or more employees who take care of accounting, marketing, and administrative matters.

Some manufacturers' and wholesale sales reps have large territories and do considerable traveling. Because a sales region may cover four or five states, they may be on the road for several days or weeks at a time.

Some rack up hundreds of airline frequent flyer miles every year. Others, who work near their home base, may do most of their traveling by car. All of them certainly cover a lot of landscape. How much of it they get to appreciate may be another matter. For busy sales reps, days can be totally occupied making sales calls and many evenings spent writing reports and taking care of records. Traveling sales reps rarely work a standard 40-hour week.

Despite their often long and hectic hours, most sales reps have some freedom in determining their own schedule. They might arrange their appointments to allow some time off when they want it—and where they want it. And dealing with the variety of people you encounter in this level of sales work can be stimulating as well as demanding.

On the demanding side of the coin, sales reps operate in a fiercely competitive world. They must compete for business not only with reps from other companies, but with other reps within their own organization. Because their incomes depend largely, and often solely, on commissions, manufacturers' reps are under pressure to maintain and expand their client bases. Their companies may offer prizes and bonuses for reaching sales goals, but they also set sales quotas, which may eventually be pushed beyond reasonable attainment levels.

Getting into the Business

Two out of three reps work in wholesale trade—mostly for distributors of machinery and equipment, food products, motor vehicles and parts, hardware, plumbing, and electrical goods. Others work for manufacturers.

Reps employed directly by manufacturers and wholesalers may be paid a base salary plus commissions. Self-employed reps usually work for a straight commission on their sales. They generally have gained experience and recognition with a manufacturer or wholesaler before going into business for themselves.

The background needed for these sales jobs varies by product line and market. Increasingly, a college degree is required, but many firms look mainly for previous sales experience. As a rule, the more sophisticated the product, the more educational preparation will be required for sales reps in that line. Firms selling industrial products may require that sales reps have a degree in science or engineering, in addition to industry work experience.

Many companies have formal training programs for beginning sales reps; they may last up to two years. Trainees might work in several jobs in the company's plants and offices to learn all phases of production, quality control, installation, and distribution. There might be classroom instruction followed by on-the-job training in branch offices under the supervision of field sales managers.

Manufacturers' reps should be goal oriented, have a persuasive but pleasant personality, and thrive on working independently. The ability to get along with people and problem-solving skills are a plus. Patience and perseverance are a must. And you should like traveling because you'll do a lot of it, visiting current and prospective clients.

Your Future as a Sales Rep

Employment of manufacturers' and wholesalers' reps should increase faster than average as the U.S. economy expands and demand for durable and nondurable goods increases. At the same time, the employment outlook will vary somewhat depending on the industry and type of sales jobs. Opportunities probably will be greatest in wholesale firms, where the majority of jobs are already, and in fields and product lines where demand is strong, such as consumer products and computers, related equipment, and supplies.

Foreign competition is increasing in most manufacturing in-dustries. As a result, firms probably will have to increase their sales forces; some will hire reps directly; others will rely more heavily on independent manufacturers' reps.

In addition to having advancement possibilities within their own firm, the regular contact sales reps have with businesspeople in other firms may open up opportunities with other employers. Some sales reps eventually move into buying, purchasing, adver-tising, or marketing research. And there is always the option to go into business for themselves.

The income of most sales reps is based on a combination of salary and commission or bonus. Commissions usually are based on the amount of sales; bonuses may be tied to individual perfor-mance, the production of all sales workers in a group or district, or on the company's performance or goals.

Median annual earnings for manufacturers' reps are about $30,800. The middle 50 percent earned between $21,900 and $45,600 a year. The top 10 percent earned more than $57,000.

Sales reps working for an employer usually are reimbursed for their travel and entertainment expenses and receive numerous benefits, including health and life insurance, a pension plan, vacation and sick leave, use of a company car, and frequent flyer mileage rewards. In addition, some companies offer incentives such as free trips or gifts for top sales performers.

Self-employed manufacturers' reps may have earnings signifi-cantly higher, or lower, than those of employee reps. It will depend on their client base and the efficiency of their own operating overhead expenses.

For more information:

Manufacturers' Agents National Association
23016 Mill Creek Road
P.O. Box 3467
Laguna Hills, CA 92654

The Merchant Marine

For a lot of young people with active imaginations, shipping out on a merchant ship to see the world ranks right up there with joining the circus. You can see the world—at least the world's port cities—as a crew member on a deep-sea merchant ship. But the view can be very limited.

A typical seagoing merchant ship has a captain, three deck officers, or mates, a chief engineer, and three assistant engineers, plus six or more deckhands and oilers. Larger vessels also have a full-time cook and helper.

The captain is master of this seagoing domain and supervises the operation of the ship and the work of the other officers and the crew. The captain is responsible for overseeing the loading and unloading of cargo or passengers, maintaining logs and other records of the ship's movements and cargo carried, and ensuring that proper procedures and safety practices are being followed at all times and that the machinery and equipment are in good working order.

Like a top boss ashore, the captain sets policy (in this case, course and speed) and designates assistants to carry out the functions necessary to achieve it.

The Work

Various members of the ship's crew steer the ship, operate the engines, signal to other vessels, maneuver to avoid hazards and other ships. They determine the ship's position using navigation aids, celestial observations, and charts. They moor or dock the vessel in port.

It sounds just like you remember seeing in those movies, but the reality today may be less exciting than shipboard action on the silver screen. Modern superships are goliaths whose momentum may carry them several miles forward after an "all stop" command. And paper charts, compasses, and sextants—while still found aboard ships—have largely given way to computerized instruments that set courses and assist with steering and engine operation.

On large vessels, captains are assisted by deck officers or mates. There might be a chief, or first, mate and second and third mates. They "stand watch" (oversee operation of the vessel) for specified periods, usually four hours on and eight off. On small ships, there may be only one mate, called a pilot on some inland vessels, who alternates watches with the captain.

Engineers (officially called marine engineers) operate, maintain, and repair propulsion engines, boilers, generators, pumps, and other machinery on a ship. There are usually four engineering officers—a chief engineer and first, second, and third assistant engineers, who stand watches in the engine compartments, overseeing operation of engines and machinery.

Able bodied deckhands help navigate and steer the ship, operate deck equipment, and keep the nonengineering areas in good condition. They look out for other vessels, obstructions in the ship's path, and aids to navigation—like buoys and lighthouses (now mostly electronic beacons). At sea there are constant maintenance chores, such as repairing hawsers (lines), chipping rust, and painting and cleaning decks and other areas. Deckhands also maintain and operate deck equipment—lifeboats, anchors, winches, cranes, and other cargo-handling gear.

When the ship is docking or departing, the deckhands secure or release the lines that hold the ship to the dock. They also work at loading and unloading cargo. On larger ships, a boatswain or head seaman directs the work of the deckhands.

In the ship's engine rooms, the equivalent of deckhands are the marine oilers. Marine oilers lubricate gears, shafts, bearings, and other moving parts of engines and motors. They monitor gauges and record data as they repair and adjust machinery.

Life at Sea

The life of a sailor is one that requires absence from home and family for extended periods. Ships might ferry cargo back and forth between several major ports, hauling crude oil between the Middle East and the U.S. or Japan, for instance. Or, ships may be assigned itineraries that have them dropping off and picking up cargo at a series of ports, often far-flung. At the end of a voyage, a ship may have circled the globe.

For long spells at sea, sailors earn long shore leaves. They might work 30 to 90 straight days and have 30 or 60 days off. Merchant marine officers and deckhands, experienced and beginners, are hired through union hiring halls or directly by shipping companies that control the ships. Generally the more seniority you have, the longer the voyage you can sign on for. Once you've signed on, you are committed to stay with the ship for that period. Except in extraordinary circumstances, such as serious illness, leaving the ship (jumping ship) before your tour is up can bring financial and other penalties. And when you join a ship in the United States, you are only to leave it in the United States.

At sea, sailors work in shifts around the clock. Typically, they work ("stand watch") for four hours, then are off for eight hours, seven days a week. They work in all weather conditions. There are hazards that can mean injury or death—fire, collision, sinking, falling overboard, or working with heavy machinery, heavy loads, and dangerous cargo.

In-port watches are eight hours on, sixteen off. The best watch is the 8 A.M. to 4 P.M. watch; that way you can spend the afternoon and evening exploring the port city.

Newer vessels are air-conditioned, soundproofed from noisy machinery, and equipped with comfortable living quarters. Even so, the long periods away from home and the confinement aboard ship send some sailors ashore for good.

The world you get to see in your travels on a merchant ship may not be quite what you imagine. Because today's merchant cargo carriers operate on tight schedules, you might not have much time ashore at the port cities you visit around the world.

A ship's typical routine is to arrive in a port and stand off its docks until space is available for the ship to dock and unload or take on cargo, which is done in the fastest possible time to make up for the waiting time at anchor. Loading operations often continue around the clock. "You might wait on the hook (at anchor) for hours or weeks," said one deckhand.

Once at the dock, huge modern container ships can be loaded and unloaded fairly quickly, perhaps within a day. It can take three or four days to load or unload ships carrying bulk cargo, such as coal and grain.

When crew members go ashore, they usually are required to stay within 25 miles of the port city. In many cases, the ship's crew has only a few hours to go ashore, and that means they can't roam far beyond the dock area, usually not the most attractive part of a city. Nevertheless, following the sea will probably always have a certain adventurous appeal.

Marcel Scuderi joined the merchant marine when he was 19, fresh out of high school and Seafarers' Union training. In the four years he served aboard merchant ships, he visited 33 countries around the world. "These were my college years," he says.

"The experience couldn't be beat. You get to travel and make pretty decent money," says Scuderi. He preferred sailing on older freighters and tankers. "They do a lot of port hopping in a region of the world, and they stay in port longer than the newer, larger ships. The first ship I was on made 11 ports in two months' time."

In his four years on various ships, Scuderi visited Russia, Germany, Belgium, India, Japan, Singapore, Hong Kong, the U.S. West Coast, and ports in Africa and the Middle East. Eventually he decided to stay ashore, went to art school, and became a graphic designer.

Getting into the Merchant Marine

Deck and engineering officers in the Merchant Marine must be licensed. To qualify for that license, applicants must have graduated from the U.S. Merchant Marine Academy at Kings Point, New York, or from one of the six state merchant marine academies. Three years of appropriate sea experience can be substituted for this schooling. All applicants also must pass a license exam.

These requirements are not met easily or quickly by most. Since sailors may actually work only six months a year, or less, racking up the requisite sea experience can take five to eight years. And the license exam is difficult to pass without substantial formal schooling or independent study.

Education and experience are important at all stages in the Merchant Marine. To advance from third officer to a higher rate also requires experience and passing scores on additional exams. Because of the stiff competition for ship's officer spots, candidates often will take a job below the one they are qualified for just to get in line for the better position.

Is just signing on and sailing off on a merchant ship still possible? In a way, it is.

To become what's called an *unlicensed seaman*—the bottom rung on the merchant marine ladder—you need a merchant mariner's document. All that is required to get it is U.S. citizenship and a U.S. Public Health Service medical certificate stating you have good color perception and are in good general physical condition. Although no experience or formal schooling is required, training at a school operated by the Seafarers' International Union of North America, AFL-CIO, can ease your way.

Applicants who are accepted are classified as *ordinary seaman* and may be assigned to the deck or engineering departments of U.S. merchant ships. With experience at sea, and more union-sponsored training, an ordinary seaman can become an *able seaman* by passing an exam.

No training, experience, or documentation is required to become a deckhand on vessels operating in U.S. harbors, rivers, and similar waterways. This is where many would-be deep-sea sailors begin to accumulate the on-the-job experience they need to eventually qualify for a merchant marine license.

Entry, training, and educational requirements for most water transportation occupations are established and regulated by the U.S. Coast Guard.

Job Outlook

The number of U.S. merchant mariners is declining. And employment will continue to fall as U.S.-staffed ships carry an ever smaller proportion of international cargo. Some say the high union wages of U.S. merchant sailors have driven ship operators to staff their ships with cheap labor crews of foreign nationals.

Whatever the reason, the decline in jobs is real and has created stiff competition for available openings. Many experienced merchant mariners go long periods without work. Unions generally are accepting fewer new members than in the past. Many Merchant Marine academy graduates have not found licensed shipboard jobs in the U.S. merchant fleet.

Merchant mariners who work full-time have median earnings of $28,680. Earnings of the middle 50 percent range from

$21,000 to $42,000. The top 10 percent, most of whom are captains or harbor pilots, earn more than $57,000.

For more information:

Maritime Administration
U.S. Department of Transportation
400 7th Street, S.W.
Washington, DC 20590

Seafarers Harry Lundeberg School of Seamanship
Route 249, St. Mary's County
Piney Point, MD 20674

CHAPTER SIX

Military and Law Enforcement Careers

The Military

As the venerable recruiting slogan says, you can see the world as a member of the U.S. armed forces. Of course, you may see it from the inside of a Bradley fighting vehicle, an F16 attack jet, or a naval ship at sea!

The mission of the armed forces is to deter aggression and defend the United States in times of conflict. In addition, the Coast Guard (under the Department of Transportation except in wartime, when it serves with the Navy) enforces federal maritime laws, rescues distressed vessels and aircraft at sea, operates aids to navigation, and battles smugglers—nowadays, largely dope runners in the rivers and coastal waters of the United States.

To perform this mission, the military stations personnel at outposts around the world, from radar stations and intelligence listening posts in remote areas of the globe to major air, land, and sea bases that circle the world at strategic locations in countries allied with the United States.

At some foreign posts, members of the military may bring their families with them. And, on their off-duty time, they may tour the region like other sightseers and holiday travelers.

The Work

Just about any kind of job that exists in civilian society also exists in the military. Military personnel run hospitals, operate nuclear reactors, drive trucks, run ships. There are doctors, lawyers, ministers, secretaries, butchers, bakers, aircraft and truck repairers in the service. Altogether, the armed forces are America's largest employer, with about 2.2 million persons on the active duty payroll in normal times. The military services provide educational opportunities and work experience in literally thousands of occupations and at every career level.

Men and women in the service hold managerial and administrative jobs; professional, technical, and clerical jobs; construction jobs; electrical and electronics jobs; mechanical and repair jobs; and many others. In addition to jobs that have an equivalent in civilian life, the armed forces have jobs that are unique to the military, such as infantry specialists, artillery gun crews, aircraft carrier catapult operators.

There are more than 2,000 basic and advanced military occupational specialties for enlisted personnel and 1,600 for officers. They include: the military jobs of infantry specialists, gun crews, and seamanship specialists who are the backbone of the services; functional support and administrative jobs that are similar to those in business and government, from personnel managers to payroll clerks; electronic equipment repairers; communications and intelligence specialists; service and supply workers; medical and dental technicians; civil engineers and architects; machinists, plumbers, welders, and other craft workers; technical and specialty occupations, from public affairs officers and band directors to photographers and graphic designers.

Of all military personnel, about 21 percent are in electrical and mechanical equipment repair; 17 percent are infantry, gun crew, and seamanship specialists; 15 percent are in functional support and administrative jobs; 10 percent in electronic equipment repair; 10 percent in communications and intelligence; 9 percent in service and supply; 6 percent in medical and dental specialties; 4 percent are craftspeople; 2 percent in other technical and allied specialties.

Officers, who account for about 14 percent of all military personnel, are concentrated in administrative, medical, and dental specialties as well as in combat activities, where they serve as ships' officers, aircraft pilots and crew members, and infantry or artillery officers.

Military life is more regimented than civilian life. Some people have trouble adapting to the military discipline; some can't take the feeling that their lives are not their own.

When you sign an enlistment contract, you sign a legal document that obligates you to serve for a specified period of time, and generally there is no backing out. Dress and grooming requirements are more stringent than in most civilian jobs, and rigid formalities govern many aspects of everyday life. For example, officers and enlisted personnel do not socialize together, and superior commissioned officers are saluted and addressed as "sir" or "ma'am." These and other rules encourage respect for superiors whose commands must be obeyed immediately and without question.

The needs of the military always come first. As a result, hours and working conditions can be quite different from the civilian workplace. As a rule, most military personnel work eight hours a day, five or five-and-a-half days a week. However, on a rotating basis, military personnel may have to work or be on call nights and weekends; it's called "having the duty." In the service, when you are called, no matter the time or day, you must respond.

Travel is part of life for all members of the service. Depending on the branch of the service and your particular job in the military, you may spend considerable time traveling. For example, the officers and crews of naval ships roam the oceans and visit ports around the world. U.S. air and ground troops stationed overseas can spend their weekends and vacation time joining other tourists visiting the countries where the military personnel have been sent as part of their jobs.

U.S. military personnel are stationed throughout the United States and in many countries around the world. More than 510,000 are stationed outside the United States. Most of these are posted in Europe, but large numbers of troops also are based in the Western Pacific region.

While military duty certainly offers an opportunity to see the world, you pay a price for that travel. Your quarters on a military ship may be rather spartan. Your port calls may be limited. You may be confined to your ship, such as a nuclear submarine, for periods of months without any port call at all. And you are separated from your family when at sea.

Air and ground forces stationed overseas may be in isolated areas, in countries where there are few amenities, or in parts of the world subject to extremes of temperature and other conditions. Overseas troops may be in hazardous situations even when combat is not involved. Of course, there is always the possibility that you'll be engaged in combat. The recent Persian Gulf War is a good example. Sometimes military training activities can be almost as dangerous.

Signing Up

Since 1973 the U.S. military has been a volunteer force. Enlisted members must sign a legal agreement that usually involves a commitment to eight years of service, with two to six of those years on active duty and the balance in the reserves. In return the service provides a job, pay (plus cash bonuses for enlistment in certain occupations), medical and other benefits, training and continuing education.

Applicants for enlistment must be under 35, pass written tests and medical exams, and have a high school diploma or equivalent for certain service options.

Officers enter the service through one of the military academies, where appointments come through members of Congress, competitive examinations, and Reserve Officer Training Corps programs at colleges and universities around the country. Upon graduation from the academies or ROTC training in college, officer candidates receive commissions in the services. College graduates who have not taken ROTC courses can apply for direct admission to the services through Officer Candidate School programs.

As military jobs become more technical and complex, educational requirements are rising. High school graduates and even those with some college background will be in demand for jobs in the enlisted ranks. Officers must have at least a four-year college degree, and certain occupational specialties require advanced degrees or degrees in particular fields.

Your Future in the Military

Job opportunities in the armed services should be excellent in all branches through the end of this century, as the prime recruitment age population declines. About 300,000 enlisted personnel and 25,000 officers are needed each year to replace those who retire or otherwise leave the armed forces.

Military personnel enjoy more job security than their civilian counterparts. And in the years ahead, more attention probably will be paid to improving the quality of military life—with such things as shorter periods of sea duty and child-care facilities at land bases—as the armed forces look for ways to improve the retention of their personnel.

Starting salaries of military enlisted personnel range from $646 to $814 a month (for those with special skills). For warrant officers, the starting pay range is $1,195 to $1,434 per month. For commissioned officers, the monthly range is $1,339 to $1,904 (for those with special skills).

In addition to their basic pay, military personnel receive free room and board, or housing and subsistence allowances, medical and dental care, a military clothing allowance, military supermarket and department store shopping privileges, 30 days of paid vacation per year, and opportunities for travel on military transportation.

The average compensation of all military personnel in 1989, including basic pay and housing and subsistence allowances, was $23,675 annually. Enlisted personnel averaged $20,524; warrant officers, $34,870; commissioned officers, $43,151.

Special pay generally is available for unusually demanding or hazardous duty, assignment to duties requiring skills in which there is a shortage, assignment to certain areas outside the continental United States, and for outstanding performance evaluations. Military personnel are eligible for retirement benefits after 20 years of service.

Other fringe benefits of the military life include athletic and other recreational facilities—such as libraries, gymnasiums, tennis courts, golf courses, bowling centers, and movie theaters—that are available at many military installations. Advice and assistance with personal or financial problems is also available through the services.

For more information:

The Department of Defense publishes a military career guide for students, and each of the service branches publishes handbooks, fact sheets, and pamphlets that describe entrance requirements, training and advancement opportunities, and other aspects of military careers. These publications are available at all recruiting stations, many state employment service offices, and in many high schools, colleges, and public libraries. Or, you can contact these offices:

Department of the Army
HQUS Army Recruiting Command
Fort Sheridan, IL 60037

U.S. Air Force Recruiting Service
Randolph AFB, TX 78150

Commandant of the Marine Corps
Headquarters
Washington, DC 20380-0001

Navy Recruiting Command
4015 Wilson Boulevard
Arlington, VA 22203-1991

Commandant (G-PRJ)
U.S. Coast Guard
Washington, DC 20590

Law Enforcement

Whether in pursuit of a wanted fugitive or of clues needed to solve a crime, law-enforcement officers may travel across the country and overseas. As you'll see in a moment, there are many branches in the field of law enforcement. Perhaps the one that springs to mind first when you are talking about travel is the highway patrol force.

State Troopers

Talk about hitting the road, state highway patrol officers do it every day. Usually called state troopers, or highway patrol officers, state police officers are responsible for patrolling state highways and federal interstates and enforcing the law within their states.

Cruising the highways that crisscross the country is not the only job of the state police, but it is probably the most visible. A state trooper's car is a welcome sight when you are stranded on the side of the road with car trouble—and an upsetting sight when you're being pulled over for speeding after zipping past an unseen radar trap.

In addition to ticketing motorists who drive too fast and recklessly, state troopers give life-saving first aid, call for emergency help and vehicles, and direct traffic at accident scenes. They also write reports that may be used to determine the cause of accidents. For highway travelers in less serious need of help, the state police can radio for road service when drivers are having mechanical trouble, direct tourists to their destinations, and occasionally provide information about the location of lodging, restaurants, and tourist attractions.

These traveling police officers also provide traffic assistance and control during road repairs, fires, and other emergencies and during special occasions, such as parades and sports events. In some states, they check the weight of commercial vehicles at highway weighing stations, conduct driver licensing examinations, and distribute public reports on highway safety.

When they're not in their cars patrolling the roads, state police officers may act as security guards for the governor and travel with the state's chief executive on all official trips in and out of the state.

In most states, state troopers also have a hand in enforcing state criminal laws. They may help city or county police track and catch lawbreakers and control civil disturbances. In communities and counties that do not have a local police force or large sheriff's department, the state police are the primary law enforcement agency, investigating crimes such as burglary, assault, and murder.

Other Officers

Detectives and special agents often go to great lengths—and travel great distances—to gather facts, collect evidence for criminal cases, conduct interviews, examine records and crime scenes, observe the activities of suspects, and participate in raids and arrests.

Those who are in a position to travel most are law- enforcement agents who operate well beyond local or state boundaries—

special agents of the Federal Bureau of Investigation (the FBI), the U.S. Customs Service, the Bureau of Alcohol, Tobacco and Firearms, and the U.S. Secret Service. These are the legendary "G men," or Government men—and women.

FBI agents investigate violations of federal law, typically bank robberies, theft of government property, organized crime, espionage, sabotage, kidnapping, terrorism. Many of these cases are international in scope. Agents with specialized training usually work on cases related to their area of expertise. For example, agents with an accounting background may investigate white collar crimes such as bank embezzlements or fraudulent bankruptcies and land deals. The agents usually are called to testify in court about the cases they investigate.

Customs agents enforce laws preventing the illegal smuggling of goods across U.S. borders. Alcohol, Tobacco and Firearms agents investigate suspected illegal sales of guns and the underpayment of federal taxes by liquor or cigarette manufacturers.

A major responsibility of the U.S. Secret Service is to protect the president and vice-president of the United States and their immediate families, as well as presidential candidates, ex-presidents, and foreign dignitaries visiting the United States. But Secret Service agents also are charged with investigating counterfeiting, forgery of government checks or bonds, and the fraudulent use of credit cards.

Obviously, Secret Service agents in the Presidential Protective Force log thousands of miles of travel every year. They must accompany the president and vice-president on their travels throughout the nation and around the world. And some squads from the presidential force travel in advance to locations the president plans to visit in order to check out potential hazards and figure out ways to avoid them.

Police and special agents usually work 40-hour weeks. On the other hand, because the services of their agencies are provided around the clock, some officers work weekends, holidays, and nights. Since police and special agents can be called to duty at any time their services are needed, they may have to work overtime, particularly during complex criminal investigations.

And, of course, the jobs of some special agents, such as those on the Secret Service's presidential squad, require extensive and far-flung travel.

Uniformed police officers, plainclothes detectives, and special agents may have to work outdoors for long periods in all kinds of weather. The injury rate among them is higher than in many other occupations, largely because of the risks involved in pursuing speeding motorists, apprehending dangerous criminals, and dealing with public disorders.

Getting into Law Enforcement

To be a police officer or special agent, you should have a sense of public service and enjoy working with many different types of people.

State police agencies employ about 10 percent of all police, detectives, and special agents. Various federal agencies—primarily the Treasury Department and the FBI—employ about 5 percent. The balance are employed by local police departments.

Civil service regulations govern the appointment of police officers in practically all states and large cities. Basically, candidates must perform well on competitive written examinations and meet requirements based on education and experience. They must also pass physical exams that test vision, strength, and agility.

Personal characteristics such as honesty, good judgment, and a sense of responsibility are especially important in police and detective work, so candidates are interviewed by a senior officer and their character traits and background are usually investigated. For some police jobs, candidates are interviewed by a psychiatrist or psychologist or are given personality tests. And most applicants are subjected to lie detector exams and drug testing.

For many police jobs, you need only a high school education. But an increasing number of cities and states require some college training for these jobs, and some hire law enforcement students as police interns. More and more police departments are encouraging applicants to take post–high school training in law enforcement. Nowadays many entrants to police and detective jobs have completed some formal postsecondary education; a significant number are college graduates.

To be considered for appointment as an FBI special agent, an applicant must be a college graduate with a major in accounting, engineering, or computer science or have a law degree or be fluent in a foreign language. College graduates who don't have specialized degrees must also have at least three years of full-time work experience.

In addition, candidates must be between 23 and 35 years old, willing to accept assignment anywhere in the United States, and be in excellent physical condition, with at least 20/200 vision corrected to 20/40 in one eye and 20/20 in the other. All new agents undergo 15 weeks of training at the FBI Academy at the U.S. Marine Corps Base in Quantico, Virginia.

Applicants for special agent jobs with the U.S. Treasury Department must have a college degree or minimum of three years work experience, at least two of which are in criminal investigation, or a comparable combination of experience and education. Candidates must be in excellent physical condition and be less than 35 years old at the time they begin duty. Treasury agents undergo eight weeks of training at the Federal Law Enforcement Training Center in Glenco, Georgia, plus eight weeks of specialized training with their particular bureau.

Your Future in the Field

Due to the increase in the country's population and need for police protection, employment of police, detectives, and special agents is expected to increase at about an average rate through the year 2000.

A more security-conscious society and growing concern about drug related crimes should contribute to heightened demand for police services workers. However, a factor that could temper employment growth somewhat is continuing budgetary constraints in local, state, and national government.

Competition will be extremely keen for special agent positions with the FBI and the U.S. Treasury Department. These prestigious jobs tend to attract a far greater number of applicants than there are openings. Consequently, only the most highly qualified candidates will win these jobs.

Earnings

A survey by the International City Management Association in 1988 showed police officers started at an average of $22,700 a year, with earnings reaching an average maximum of $29,400 a year after about six years of service. Actual salaries can vary, depending on the area of the country and the size of the city or town worked.

According to an earlier study by the Bureau of Justice Statistics, police and detective sergeants earned salaries ranging from $17,500 in jurisdictions of fewer than 2,500 people to $35,300 in jurisdictions of greater than a million population. Salaries for police chiefs range from about $19,000 to $87,000 in the larger jurisdictions.

Starting FBI agents earn about $26,300 a year. Starting U.S. Treasury Department agents earn about $15,700 to $19,500 a year. Experienced FBI agents earn around $41,100, and supervisory agents receive about $48,600 a year. Salaries of experienced U.S. Treasury Department agents start at $34,600, while supervisory agents start at $41,100.

For more information:

If you're interested in becoming a local or state police officer, contact local and state police departments and civil service commissions.

FBI
Applicant Recruiting Office
1900 Half Street, S.W.
Washington, DC 20535

Pamphlets with general information about jobs as special agents with the U.S. Department of the Treasury are available from any U.S. Office of Personnel Management Job Information Center (listed in phone directories under U.S. Government, Office of Personnel Management).

CHAPTER SEVEN

Representing the United States Abroad

Join the Peace Corps

Since President John F. Kennedy created the Peace Corps in 1961, American volunteers have been sharing their skills and energy with people in the poorer areas of the world—the so-called developing countries.

The Peace Corps mission is to promote world peace and friendship—by helping the people of interested countries meet their needs for trained men and women and by encouraging better mutual understanding between people in the United States and those in the countries the Peace Corps serves.

At the invitation of host governments, about 6,000 Peace Corps volunteers now serve in 66 countries. The Peace Corps is the only U.S. government agency that places its people in communities to live and work directly with the people of developing nations.

The Peace Corps volunteers have made many friends for the United States by demonstrating that they personally care about their host country communities—care enough to spend two years of their lives working directly with the people to make life better.

As a Peace Corps volunteer, you will travel—primarily to the underdeveloped areas of the world. And during your service, usually two years, you are encouraged to use your vacation time to further explore the country where you are stationed.

Life in the Peace Corps

Peace Corps volunteers work side by side with host country co-workers to make things happen—useful, appropriate, and lasting things. The projects they work on are determined by the communities where volunteers are stationed. The Peace Corps volunteer's mission is not to do things for people, but to help people do things for themselves.

For example, volunteers are teaching farmers in several African countries how to cultivate tilapia, a fish that tolerates bad water, consumes insects and agricultural by- products, and reproduces every three months. Tilapia is a rich source of protein. African farmers who recognize its value can pass the technology on to other generations by instructing their children in the cultivation of tilapia.

Peace Corps volunteers helped the people of Mali establish a local soap-making factory, where villagers can earn cash incomes. In Nepal, a volunteer at a school for the deaf has helped develop the first sign language dictionary in Nepali. Volunteers have introduced science and business curricula in the Kingdom of Tonga, shown Paraguayan farmers how to stop soil erosion, taught Ghanaian students masonry techniques, designed water supply systems in Belize, and helped develop disease-resistant vegetables in Western Samoa.

Before serving in the Peace Corps, many would-be volunteers think that physical hardship will be the most difficult part of the experience. In hindsight, however, most of them see things differently. The most common difficulty they report is adapting to the slow pace at which change occurs. Many volunteers see a huge gap between the existing situation and the potential for transforming it. The larger the gap, the greater the level of frustration. To bring about change that will remain after the volunteer returns home may be the most challenging aspect of Peace Corps service.

Says one Peace Corps veteran, "I would and have advised other people, including my mother, to join the Peace Corps. I wouldn't, however, advise everyone to join because the experience is not for everyone."

"I believe you have to be adventurous, very adaptable, and really want to be where you are," says this volunteer. "The most difficult part for me has been being apart from family and friends."

But another returned worker says, "I intend to join the Peace Corps again after I retire. I fell in love, I fell sick, I fell off my mule (twice), and, most of all, I fell for my town. Peace Corps gives you a healthy dose of how the majority of people in the world live."

Most Peace Corps assignments are for two years and begin after the completion of training. Vacation time is accrued at two days per month, and volunteers are encouraged to use it for travel in their host country.

Training sessions usually take between 8 and 14 weeks and are most often held in the host countries. Volunteers are expected to speak the language of the people with whom they live and work, so language instruction is intense during this period. Instructors are host country nationals, often with years of experience working with Peace Corps volunteers. The training includes in-depth orientation to the culture and traditions of the host country and technical instruction to help you adapt your skills to your particular overseas assignments.

Volunteers work for a government department, agency, or organization in the host country. They are supervised by, and work with, host country nationals, and they are subject to local laws.

Getting into the Peace Corps

Any healthy adult U.S. citizen is eligible to apply for the Peace Corps. Married couples are welcome if both can work and are qualified to be volunteers. Blacks and other minorities are especially sought for Peace Corps assignments, and older persons are also welcome. Although fewer than 10 percent of Peace Corps volunteers are 50 years old and older, host country governments say they want more older Americans as volunteers. Many societies overseas place high value on age and associate it with wisdom.

For many assignments, knowledge of a language other than English is necessary. Previous fluency in that language can be very helpful, but is not always required. Peace Corps training includes intensive language instruction.

To be accepted to a Peace Corps assignment, your skills must match the criteria requested by host countries for particular programs. These criteria vary with different areas. Most require a four-year college degree or three to five years of relevant work experience. Community service and your character and personality are also factors in selection. The Peace Corps looks for people with perseverance, adaptability, creativity in problem solving, and sociability.

Specialties generally in demand include agriculturalists, natural resources managers, and teacher trainers. Liberal arts generalists are welcome and can help on projects as diverse as fish farming, beekeeping, health and nutrition and other community services, and general leadership and organizing. Fishery specialists, engineers, businesspeople (especially those who can help developers of small business enterprises and cooperatives), nurses and other health professionals, home economists, skilled tradespeople, and educators are also encouraged to volunteer.

Apply to join the Peace Corps at least nine months prior to the time you'll be available. You must be ready to begin service within one year of submitting application forms. In some cases, it is possible to leave for training as early as three months after your application is received.

Selection for a Peace Corps assignment comes only after you have been invited to enter a training program and successfully complete it.

Your Future in the Peace Corps

Most Peace Corps assignments last just two years, beginning after your completion of training. In order to complete a particular project or activity, volunteers may request an extension of service, which must be approved by the country director.

During your two years, all expenses related to your service— travel, health care and insurance, housing, vacation (45 days during the two years), and monthly living expenses (paid in the local currency for food, clothing, household, and incidental expenses)—are provided by the Peace Corps. And when you have completed your assignment, you will receive a readjustment allowance of $200 for every month you served—$4,800 for a two-year tour.

In the Peace Corps, you receive full health benefits. Trainees must pass rigorous medical examinations and receive immunizations and health training before they leave the United States, and they will not be sent to countries where their health needs cannot be met. The Peace Corps maintains a medical staff in most countries. Where there is not a staff, local health professionals are fully trained, and there are facilities equipped to handle emergencies. If medical problems occur that cannot be treated locally, the volunteer is sent to a modern facility in another country or back to the United States.

Every effort is made to ensure the safety of Peace Corps volunteers. Each Peace Corps post overseas has an emergency plan for coping with natural disasters or other threats to volunteers' health and well-being.

Can you choose where you want to serve? Possibly. The application form allows you to indicate area preferences as well as those places where you do not wish to serve. You will not be assigned to a country or region where you do not want to go. To be sent to a particular country, however, a volunteer must have a skill currently being requested by that country. If you are only willing to serve in one country or area, your chances of being accepted are limited. Personal flexibility with regard to assignments is very important to help the Peace Corps fill the requests of many host countries.

In most locations, you will work in collaboration with a host country national assigned to the same project. Another Peace Corps volunteer may be posted in a nearby village or town. In larger urban areas, of course, a number of Peace Corps volunteers working on a variety of projects may reside in the same area.

Living situations vary enormously from one country to another and depending on the nature of the program. Many volunteers live in cement, brick, or adobe houses. Generally the more rural the program, the more basic the housing will be. In urban areas, volunteers' quarters often have running water and electricity. Most volunteers live comfortably, but very modestly.

Your future as a Peace Corps volunteer is mostly beyond your service in the corps. When Peace Corps volunteers return home, their experience can help shape their future. The benefits of two years in the Peace Corps include great personal growth, a new perspective on the world, travel, and a greater understanding of how the United States is perceived by other cultures.

There are also specific career benefits: language and skills training, hands-on experience in the developing world, and some specially created career and educational opportunities. For instance, more than 50 graduate schools provide scholarships for returned volunteers. In some states, overseas teaching experience may be substituted for practice teaching requirements necessary for professional accreditation as a teacher. And for qualified persons in certain disciplines, such as forestry and soil science, National Direct Student Loans may be available with substantially reduced repayments and interest canceled in return for a full two years of Peace Corps service.

Says a Peace Corps veteran: "I could come up with a long list of ex-volunteers scattered among banking, finance, international trade, and development agencies who are reaching mid-level and, in some cases, senior positions. When you put us all together, we're becoming a pretty influential group, particularly in regard to Africa and other developing regions."
For more information:

U.S. Peace Corps
P-301
Washington, DC 20526

Or call toll free 1-800-424-8580, extension 93, to locate the recruitment office for your area.

Join the U.S. Foreign Service

The very title Foreign Service conjures up exotic images of travel to faraway places. It may not live up to the wildest of those images, but it is a career field where travel and living in foreign destinations is a routine part of your work.

A career in the Foreign Service is more than just a job. It is a way of life that requires a special commitment to representing the United States to the people of other countries. A Foreign Service career can bring hardships and challenges, but it can also bring you excitement, glamour, unique rewards, and exceptional professional and personal opportunities. First and foremost, you'll have the personal satisfaction of serving your country and representing America's interests—and caring for the needs of American citizens—in other countries around the world.

There are two types of career paths in the Foreign Service. One is that of Foreign Service officers (FSOs), generalists who perform administrative, consular, economic, and political functions. The other is that of Foreign Service specialists who perform technical, support, and administrative services. Employees on both tracks work at embassies and posts around the world as well as in Washington, D.C..

Many Foreign Service officers occasionally experience the glamour of dinner with their ambassador as guests in a Middle Eastern palace or the excitement of being involved in preparations for a summit meeting of international heads of state. But for the most part, the day-to-day routine of the FSO is much like that of other white-collar managers and administrators. A significant difference between work in the Foreign Service and that in other branches of government is its location.

The FSO may work in lively Western European or Asian capitals or in the hostile climate of Antarctica or the depressing environment of a remote refugee camp in a Third World country. Many overseas posts are in remote locations where harsh climates and health hazards prevail and where American-style amenities may be hard to come by. Service at some Foreign Service posts may entail security risks for FSOs and their families.

That's why a decision to join the Foreign Service requires unusual motivation and a firm dedication to serve the public and defend and advance U.S. interests abroad. The Foreign Service officer can help shape U.S. policy by providing accurate analysis and advice based on experience and by providing dissenting views when warranted.

At the same time, FSOs must accept political and policy direction from the president's administration and direct their efforts to making those policies succeed. In a field as potentially controversial as foreign affairs, the professional Foreign Service officer is expected to place loyalty and willingness to follow instructions above personal opinions and preferences.

In many ways, FSOs are to foreign affairs what military officers are to defense. FSOs work closely with members of the civil and military services and take their policy instructions from political appointees. They can be sent anywhere in the world, at any time, to serve the diplomatic needs of the United States. They are truly the front line personnel of all U.S. embassies, consulates, and other diplomatic missions and may also be assigned to other civilian and military agencies to help them carry out their foreign policy missions.

In general, Foreign Service employees are rotated to new assignments every two to four years. During their careers, they'll live overseas about 60 percent of the time. In most circumstances, the government will cover the expense of spouses, children under 21, and dependent parents who wish to accompany an FSO to foreign posts. Security concerns and the lack of adequate educational or health facilities at some posts may deter families from accompanying Foreign Service employees to some overseas posts.

The Work

In addition to its embassies in other national capitals, the United States maintains consulates general or consulates in many other foreign cities. These are the branch offices of embassies. Primarily responsible for serving and protecting the millions of Americans who live, work, and travel abroad, these consular posts issue visas and passports and provide the embassy with political and economic reporting from their region. In all, the U.S. State Department operates more than 250 posts overseas

For many years, FSOs were viewed as generalists who, like career military officers, were assigned to various jobs in different parts of the world throughout their careers. Most FSOs still are generalists. Yet, just as the military is now attracting a new breed of officers who are more likely to be specialists, the Foreign Service is seeking candidates interested in more than political science or diplomatic history. From now into the twenty-first century, according to Secretary of State James A. Baker III, transnational issues will characterize diplomacy. Among these issues are science and technology (including the global fight against diseases such as AIDS and efforts to save the environment), antinarcotics efforts, and international trade. So the

Foreign Service seeks officers who can specialize in dealing with U.S. diplomacy in these areas.

Duties of Foreign Service Officers

Here are the kinds of work FSOs do in posts around the world:

ADMINISTRATION. FSOs are responsible for all support operations of an overseas post—hiring foreign national personnel, assuring reliable communications with Washington, overseeing sophisticated computer systems, managing the post's financial operations, providing office and residential space, assuring the best possible security for the post's personnel and property. Competent administration is critically important, especially in hostile areas.

CONSULAR SERVICES. In solving the vast range of human problems they encounter every day, consular services employees need the combined skills of social worker, lawyer, judge, investigator, and even mortician. Consular functions range from the mundane—issuing passports, visas, and federal benefits payments—to the extraordinary, such as finding a lost traveler or investigating the safety of a child involved in a custody dispute.

ECONOMIC ANALYSIS. The economic staff at embassies and consular posts deals with matters ranging from commercial aviation safety, fishing rights, and international lending practices to scientific cooperation and the environmental impact of economic development. From their contact with key foreign business and financial leaders, these FSOs prepare reports on local economic conditions and their impact on American trade and investment policies.

POLITICAL AFFAIRS. Political analysis and reporting on the views of political opponents, as well as foreign government officials, are necessary to assess the impact of U.S. policies in other countries. Political affairs FSOs cultivate contacts among labor unions, social and humanitarian organizations, local educators, and cultural leaders, all of whom may provide clues to future domestic and foreign policy shifts in the host country.

INFORMATION AND CULTURAL AFFAIRS. FSOs of the U.S. Information Agency (USIA) manage cultural, informational, and public diplomacy programs at U.S. posts overseas. For example, a USIA information officer might arrange briefings, interviews, press conferences, and other media activities to boost understanding and support for U.S. programs. A cultural affairs officer administers educational exchange programs and coordinates U.S. cultural and sports presentations.

COMMERCIAL AND BUSINESS SERVICES. An FSO working for the U.S. and Foreign Commercial Service (FCS) of the Department of Commerce identifies overseas business connections for American exporters and investors, conducts market research for American products, and organizes trade promotion events. These officers must combine the skills of an analyst and a broker with the imagination of an entrepreneur to enhance opportunities for American trade across the seas.

Duties of Foreign Service Specialists

Foreign Service specialists work at the same posts as FSOs, around the world. They deal with functions that range from telecommunications, financial, information, and personnel management to security, medical, and secretarial operations. Their job descriptions are as follows.

GENERAL SERVICES OFFICERS. These specialists manage physical resources and logistical functions at Foreign Service posts, everything from procurement of supplies to transportation and building maintenance.

FINANCIAL MANAGEMENT OFFICERS.   These officers work on the financial operations of overseas posts.

PERSONNEL OFFICERS.   The Foreign Service employs people to manage personnel services at overseas posts.

SECRETARIES.   The Foreign Service always needs people to perform secretarial and related duties.

MEDICAL OFFICERS.   These officers provide health care to U.S. government employees and dependents, evaluate local medical care facilities and advise on local community health problems, and arrange for emergency medical evacuations. Also supporting the medical program are medical technologists and nurse practitioners.

COMMUNICATIONS ELECTRONICS OFFICERS.   Their job is to handle operation and maintenance of communications equipment (radio, telephone, digital communications) at diplomatic and consular posts.

DIPLOMATIC SECURITY OFFICERS.   They are responsible for the security of U.S. facilities, operations, and personnel abroad. They perform investigative and protective work to deal with criminal, intelligence, and terrorist activities that might threaten American lives and property.

SECURITY ENGINEERING OFFICERS.   These officers conduct technical security surveys and inspections and maintain security equipment used at diplomatic and consular posts.

BUILDING AND MAINTENANCE SPECIALISTS.   They are responsible for the maintenance and repair of U.S. government-owned and government-leased property abroad.

Construction Engineers.   They supervise contractors to ensure proper building of new properties or improvements to existing ones.

Maintenance Technicians.   These technicians provide facilities maintenance such as electrical power and heating, ventilating and air conditioning.

Getting into the Foreign Service

Applicants for FSO and specialist positions must be U.S. citizens, at least 21 years old at the time of employment, pass a medical exam, have an appropriate educational background for the position (from a high school diploma to university degrees and professional licenses), and be available for assignment anywhere in the world.

Openings for specialists are listed and described in vacancy announcements, which you can request from the State Department. They note specific job requirements. The process of applying for a job can take from six months to a year. Your completed application paperwork is reviewed by a screening panel. If you pass this review, you'll be invited to an interview, usually in Washington, D.C.. If you pass the interview stage, you'll be subject to a thorough background investigation. You'll also be required to take a preemployment drug screening exam. (Once hired, all Foreign Service employees are subject to random drug testing).

The purpose of the background investigation is to determine your eligibility for a security clearance as well as your general suitability for the Foreign Service. The investigation covers such matters as registration for Selective Service, repayment of federally-guaranteed student loans, credit and tax history, employment records, drug or alcohol abuse. Investigators may interview your current and previous employers, co-workers, contacts, and neighbors. Depending on your work history, places of residence, and travels, the background check can take several months.

If you get through these initial stages and you are applying for a specialist job, your name will be placed on a register for a maximum of 18 months. Candidates for jobs are hired from the register as openings become available.

The entry screening process for Foreign Service officers includes a written examination as well as an interview- assessment. Success on both of these requires a strong command of English.

Although no specific educational background is stipulated, most successful FSO candidates have at least a bachelor's degree and a broad knowledge of international and domestic political affairs, U.S. and world history, government and foreign policy, and culture. In recent years, about 65 percent of FSO candidates had advanced degrees in international relations, economics, business administration, law, journalism, or other disciplines. Many have had work experience in various fields before their appointments.

Before accepting any Foreign Service job, you must agree to be available for assignment worldwide. Factors that will determine where you'll be sent include the need at a particular post for certain skills and specializations as well as personal preferences. Medical clearance for overseas duty is required for candidates and their dependents.

Your Future in the Foreign Service

FSO applicants who pass the initial tests and assessments and receive security and medical clearances can be hired as FSO career candidates. During a five-year probationary period, they'll be reviewed for tenure and commissioning as Foreign Service officers, usually by the fourth year. A probationary candidate who fails to perform satisfactorily during this period can be fired.

When hired for a Foreign Service specialist job, applicants become career candidates for a probationary period not to exceed four years. During that time they will be considered for tenure;

if they don't make it on the first review, they'll have another chance 12 months later. If they don't get tenure then, they'll have to leave the Foreign Service.

When you enter the Foreign Service, you receive several weeks of basic training in Washington, D.C. at the State Department's Foreign Service Institute. Initial training usually includes orientation to the Foreign Service, study about the area where you're to be posted, training in your job field, and some foreign language study. For some Foreign Service employees, the training can take up to seven months prior to the first overseas assignment, most of it involving language instruction.

Entering FSOs who already are professionally competent in a foreign language may get through this part of the training in relatively short order. It is not absolutely necessary that you know a foreign language when you apply for the Foreign Service. At the same time, if you have a demonstrated aptitude in learning foreign languages, that will be a plus for you, as all FSOs must learn a foreign language before they receive tenure in the service.

Most Foreign Service career candidates will be assigned abroad following their training in Washington. They should expect to serve a minimum of one year performing consular work some time during their first two tours of duty. Subsequent assignments will depend on their interests and functional specialization and the needs of the service.

The Foreign Service needs qualified men and women who want to serve their country in this capacity. The service especially seeks persons from varied ethnic and racial backgrounds from all regions of the United States to reflect the great diversity of the American people. Salaries are comparable to those of other federal government employees in similar job areas. Entering FSOs start at junior grades FS-5 and FS-6, with starting salaries between $23,000 and $28,000, depending on their background and experience.

In addition, Foreign Service salaries may be enhanced for workers stationed overseas, by such benefits as the shipment of household furnishings and cars to your overseas posts; travel and lodging payments while en route; government- provided housing, furniture, and utilities overseas; home leave (including travel expenses); and medical benefits. There are also educational allowances and travel for dependent children, cost of living allowances to help cover extra expenses in high-cost foreign cities, and special pay for danger and hardship posts.

As a Foreign Service employee, you will be transferred routinely according to the needs of the service. And you may have little control over where you are assigned, but as you gain experience and contacts, you may influence where you will be posted.

For more information:

Application forms and information are available from:

Recruitment Division
U.S. Department of State
Box 9317
Arlington, VA 22209
or call 703-875-7495 or 1-800-JOB-OVER.

Also look for information at college and university placement offices and regional offices of the federal government's Office of Personnel Management.

CHAPTER EIGHT

Glamour Industries

Musicians and Dancers

Of professional entertainers, the ones we most often think of as travelers are the musical performers. Even in a world of tapes, CDs, and other recorded forms of music, musicians take to the road to bring their talents to audiences in every nook and cranny of the country. Nothing beats live music.

For big rock bands, major concert tours are often an annual event. The release of a new album may kick off a cross- country or world performance tour, and another album may result from recordings during the live concerts. Country- and-western bands spend so much time on the road that many of them have their own customized buses. Willie Nelson's "On the Road Again" is the anthem of the country bands. Even symphony orchestras and ensembles take their music to other cities.

And when musicians travel, they are usually accompanied by their bands and backup singers, dancers and warm-up bands, and other show technicians, such as lighting and sound experts.

The Musician's Life

Look around. Listen. Almost every kind of music is available to you on the radio and in recordings—rock, gospel, country and western, classical, pop, rhythm and blues, jazz, zydeco, salsa, reggae. There is a vast audience for music of all kinds. In every city and hamlet, you can usually find places to listen to live music.

Singers and instrumental musicians generally work nights and weekends. That's when most performances are held. When they're not on stage, of course, musicians spend a lot of time practicing. And because many musicians earn money from their music only on a part-time basis, they may have to squeeze their rehearsal time in between nonmusical jobs from which they really earn a living.

The top traveling bands and musical groups usually work out of major entertainment and recording centers—New York, Los Angeles, Nashville, Miami, New Orleans, Detroit. And there are more than 1,600 professional orchestras and small chamber music groups in the United States, many of which travel for part of the year.

Some musicians' road trips can be a real grind. Like the classic one-night gigs in one-horse towns: The bus pulls into town several hours before a performance. The musicians scramble to freshen up and practice. An hour after the last encore, they're back in the bus on the way to the next town circled on their map. That's certainly no way to appreciate your travels.

But other musical groups travel on a saner schedule. They may spend several days or a week at cities on their itinerary, with time for sight-seeing and sampling local restaurants. Musicians, dancers, and other variety entertainers also take occasional bookings on cruise ships, which travel the Caribbean and Mexico's Pacific coast. During the day, these entertainers get to recreate with the ship's passengers.

Getting into the Field

Like actors, musicians and dancers usually begin working when they are very young, and their success will depend to a great extent on their natural talent. Their search for chances to perform before audiences, to be seen and heard, and perhaps discovered, is very much akin to the career pursuits of actors.

Because musicians perform mostly in evening sessions at clubs and concert halls, many hold jobs during the day to earn enough to survive on until they can make a living from their music. For country music performers especially, Nashville, Tennessee, is what Hollywood and New York are for actors. It's where you go to have the best chance to be noticed by the key people in the business. In Nashville, because so many people there are pursuing a musical career dream, a common question when people meet is, "What's your day job?"

Musicians also work their way into paying jobs by auditioning for spots in musical shows at major entertainment complexes, such as Walt Disney World in Florida and Disneyland in California, Opryland in Nashville, and the Busch Gardens theme parks around the country. Regional influences are strong in American music, and in addition to music industry centers like Nashville and Los Angeles, other cities with recording studios and other music businesses are magnets to aspiring musicians.

In show business, of course, performers' earnings ultimately depend on their professional reputation. Musicians hired for jobs in the movie or TV business, and by recording companies, typically earn a minimum of about $167 to $220 for a three-hour studio session. A minimum wage for a principal singer on a TV show would be about $536 for a one- hour production. But star singers and instrumentalists can command much more for each performance. Often, they perform a song or two on a TV show more for publicity and exposure than for the money.

Minimum salaries in the 21 American symphony orchestras with the largest budgets ranged from $685 to $1,065 per week during the 1988–89 season. A typical season for these orchestras can be anywhere from 47 to 52 weeks, so these are truly annual salaries. In the next tier of orchestras, salaries ranged from $469 to $960 per week for an average 41-week season. The great majority of orchestras, of course, have pay scales lower than these.

Dancers may belong to the American Guild of Musical Artists, AFL-CIO, or other unions, which establish minimum wage scales. For example, in 1989–90 the minimum pay for new dancers in ballet and modern productions was $445 a week or $198 per performance and $140 per rehearsal. On tour dancers receive additional amounts for room and board. Minimum rates for dancers on TV range from $536 to $575 for a one-hour show.

For more information:

American Federation of Musicians
1501 Broadway
New York, NY 10036

American Guild of Musical Artists
1727 Broadway
New York, NY 10019

American Symphony Orchestra League
777 14th Street, N.W., Suite 500
Washington, DC 20005

National Association of Schools of Music
11250 Roger Bacon Drive
Reston, VA 22091

National Dance Association
1900 Association Drive
Reston, VA 22091

American Dance Guild
33 W. 21st Street
New York, NY 10010

Show Business

Touring companies of actors and stage technicians are a tradition of the theater. Performers with popular shows can easily spend the better part of a year on the road. Now motion picture actors and actresses also spend a lot of time traveling.

Movies aren't just a hometown Hollywood industry anymore. In another generation, most movies were made totally on Hollywood sound stages—huge buildings the size of an aircraft hangar where scenes of offices, homes, factory floors, city streets, and even jungles and mountaintops can be replicated for scenes in movies. Now major motion picture producers tend to look for the real thing as a backdrop, no matter where on earth it is.

More and more nowadays, moviemakers take to the road in the quest for locations for their films. You'll find movies being made in little towns in North Carolina and Louisiana, on the streets of Chicago, New York, Washington, and Toronto.

Motion picture assistance offices in many states and cities offer incentives to filmmakers to attract them to their locations. Making a movie can bring jobs to local actors and would-be actors who might get roles as "extras," and it brings business to local carpenters, rental equipment companies, restaurants and caterers, hotels and other firms.

Even movies filmed in Hollywood shoot scenes on locations all around the Los Angeles area. A tour company in Hollywood sells maps and schedules of location shooting by film companies every day in Southern California, so movie fans can watch movies being made and maybe catch a glimpse of a star.

So actors and actresses, directors, producers, cinematographers, and the dozens of other kinds of workers involved in the production of movies and stage plays are frequent travelers. Read the fan magazines and entertainment columns for their itineraries—Kevin Costner is filming in a cornfield in Iowa, then in Mexico with Anthony Quinn, next on the plains of Montana. Julia Roberts is in Georgia, then New York. Tyne Daly is touring with her new play. Actors are off to Yugoslavia, Italy, wherever the scenery fits the movie script, and to theaters in hundreds of communities across the United States.

How and Where Actors Work

Acting requires persistence, practice, and hard work, as well as a special talent. Only a handful of actors and actresses achieve recognition as stars on stage and screen. A somewhat larger number are well-known, experienced performers who frequently appear in movies, plays, and television productions.

But most actors struggle for even a toehold in this profession, picking up parts wherever they can get them. It's an unsteady career; the majority of actors experience frequent periods of unemployment.

Many hold temporary jobs as waiters, salespeople, or file clerks so they can make time to go to casting calls and make the rounds in pursuit of acting jobs. Some actors teach acting courses in schools and community workshops.

Beginning actors usually start in bit parts with just a few speaking lines. They hope critics, agents, and producers will notice them and call with offers of larger supporting roles. In the theater, rookie actors may serve as understudies for the principal actors in a play. They actually play the role if the principal is sick or must be away from the production for a day or two. In film and TV, actors may hope to move from roles in commercials to movies or TV series. Successful versatile actors who can manage to play a variety of roles in movie and stage productions usually stay busy.

Actors work at odd hours. Plays are performed mostly in the evenings. Filming for the movies or TV shows may begin early in the morning and go on well into the night, especially when the crew is at a special location, where the work must be done while the light and weather and other circumstances are right for the scene.

Good performances by actors require tedious memorizing of lines and repetitive rehearsals of action. It takes physical stamina to stand the heat of stage and studio lights, the long irregular hours, and adverse weather or living conditions that may exist on location. But oh, the chance to be a star!

Some actors eventually become directors. Directors direct. That is, they show and tell actors how to interpret plays or scripts. Directors can become as famous as the stars they direct. Nearly every movie fan knows who Stephen Spielberg is. The late David Lean was known for his classics *Bridge on the River Kwai* and *Doctor Zhivago*.

Directors usually are in charge of the entire cast and crew on a movie or stage production. They conduct auditions and rehearsals and select cast members. They usually approve scenery and costumes, music and choreography. They use their knowledge of acting and the medium in which they are working to pull the best possible performances from their actors.

Getting Started

Actors usually try to get into the business at an early age. They get the acting bug in high school or college plays or summer theater and keep plugging away to make it to the big time. To gain experience, they may seek every opportunity to work in local, little theater groups and in dinner theater productions, where they wait tables during intermissions.

To hone their acting skills, they may take formal training at dramatic arts schools in New York or Los Angeles or at colleges and universities around the country.

There are no particular training requirements for directors. Some come to directing from long careers as successful actors. Some start out as directors, having learned the craft in film schools in New York or Los Angeles, or in college programs. Would-be directors who have a bachelor's degree or two years of on-the-set experience in motion picture or television production may qualify for the assistant directors training program of the Directors Guild of America and cooperating movie and television companies. To qualify you must take a written test and go through a series of group and individual assessments. Of the thousand or so applicants every year, only eight to fifteen are selected.

For most actors and directors, career advancement comes with a growing reputation for success—artistic and at the box office. Actors and directors whose work can assure that a play or movie will make money are besieged with offers of bigger and better roles and movie projects.

Your Future in Acting

Jobs for actors and others in the industry are expected to grow faster than average in the years ahead because the number of theatrical, motion picture, and television productions should continue to grow. This growth will be fueled by rising foreign demand for American productions and expanding domestic demand from the cable television, home movie rental, and TV syndication industries.

The market for live stage productions will continue to be strong in the future, as many people prefer live theater entertainment for its excitement and aesthetics. Attendance at live theater performances will continue to increase as regional and touring shows reach audiences in more and more cities outside the traditional center of theater in New York City.

That's the good news. The bad news for actors is that with the always huge number of people who want to be stars and the lack of formal entry procedures and requirements, competition for acting and directing jobs will always be fierce. Only the most talented and tenacious will be able to grab the brass ring and find steady employment in show business.

For those who do, the rewards can be modest, or they can be stratospheric. Most show business workers belong to guilds or unions that negotiate minimum wage scales with production companies. The Actors' Equity Association represents stage actors; the Screen Actors Guild and Screen Extras Guild represent actors in movies, television, and commercials; the American

Federation of Television and Radio Artists (AFTRA) represents performers in these media. Most stage directors belong to the Society of Stage Directors and Choreographers; film and TV directors belong to the Directors Guild of America.

For actors in Broadway productions, the minimum wage is $800 a week; in small off-Broadway theaters, it is $280 to $505 a week. Actors on the road in companies of stage shows can add $74 a day to their minimum wage. Eight performances comprise a week's work on the stage, and additional performances bring overtime pay. Actors may work long hours during rehearsals, but once their show opens, they work more regular hours, about 24 hours a week.

The Guild minimum for motion picture actors is $448 a day, or $1,135 for three days or $1,558 for a five-day week. For extras, the minimum is $99 a day. TV actors also receive additional compensation for reruns of their shows.

Because they work so irregularly, most actors earn pitiful amounts from their craft in the course of a year. A study showed that in one recent year about 23,000 actors had no earnings from acting; 4,500 made less than $2,500; about 6,300 earned $5,000 or more; only 675 earned more than $35,000. And from Screen Actors Guild statistics comes this dismal picture: in a year's time, more than 80 percent of all performers who worked under SAG contracts earned less than $5,000 from acting jobs, and 29 percent earned no income at all from acting. It's no wonder that many actors must supplement their acting income by holding down other jobs.

Salaries for stage directors on Broadway are about $20,000 for a rehearsal period, which usually lasts five weeks. In small dinner theaters and summer stock companies, directors earn only $500 to $600 a week, but this is where most of the jobs are.

Of course, through their agents, successful actors and directors negotiate deals for themselves with movie and show producers and companies. These deals may result in payment that can far surpass the union negotiated wages.

For more information:

Actors' Equity Association
165 W. 46th Street
New York, NY 10036

Directors Guild of America
Training Program
14144 Ventura Boulevard
Sherman Oaks, CA 91423

Become an Astronaut

The twenty-first century promises the reality of humans living and working in space. The United States, with its international partners Canada, Japan, and the European Space Agency, hopes to have Space Station Freedom operating by the late 1990s. From that orbiting depot, humans will continue their journeys to the moon and Mars. As these plans move toward reality, the need for qualified space-flight professionals will increase.

Talk about travel! Some of the trips planned for future astronauts may take years to complete.

Early in the twenty-first century, the United States intends to return to the moon, from where astronauts will voyage off to the planet Mars. The specifics have yet to be worked out, but by comparison this effort is likely to dwarf the Apollo program, which first sent astronauts to the moon.

Our first lunar base will be a spartan outpost where, in addition to venturing outside to conduct forays themselves, astronauts will probably control an army of versatile robotic workers and explorers. Meanwhile, automated spacecraft will probe Mars to pave the way for the first human visitors who will arrive sometime between 2010 and 2020.

Whether that arrival is in a solitary spaceship or with an international fleet of vessels adorned with many national symbols, humans will have begun their slow but inevitable expansion to the other planets of the Solar System. The scope of space exploration has broadened exponentially since the first U.S. manned space flight in 1961.

In seeking its first astronauts, the National Aeronautics and Space Administration (NASA) required jet aircraft flight experience and engineering training. Astronauts could be no more than 5 feet 11 inches tall because of limited cabin space in the Mercury space capsule then being designed. As America's first astronauts, NASA selected seven men from an original field of 500 candidates. They became almost legendary figures: Scott Carpenter, Gordon Cooper, Gus Grissom, Deke Slyton, John Glenn, Wally Schirra and Alan Shepard.

In 1962, 9 more pilot astronauts were chosen; in 1963, 14 more. Then, in 1964, the first 6 scientist astronauts were selected. They were chosen on the basis of educational background alone—each of them had a doctorate or equivalent experience in the natural sciences, medicine, or engineering. NASA chose 19 more pilot astronauts in 1966 and 11 more scientist astronauts in 1967.

Those who stand out in the astronaut corps, beyond the original seven, are Neil Armstrong, Buzz Aldrin, and Michael Collins, who flew the first moon-landing mission. Armstrong and Aldrin were the first men to walk on the moon, while Collins controlled the spaceship that would return the three astronauts to earth.

By 1978 the first group of astronaut candidates for the Space Shuttle program were selected. There were 20 mission specialists and 15 pilots who completed training and became active-status astronauts in that class. Six of them were women, and four were members of minorities. Additional groups of pilots and mission specialists were added to the astronaut corps through the 1980s.

Earthbound Life

Astronaut candidates receive training at the Johnson Space Center near Houston, Texas. They attend classes in basic science and technology, including mathematics, Earth resources, meteorology, guidance and navigation, astronomy, physics, and computers. Candidates also receive training in space suits, the use of space tools, parachute jumping, and land and sea survival procedures.

They are exposed to problems associated with high (hyperbaric) and low (hypobaric) atmospheric pressures in altitude chambers. They also experience the microgravity of space flight; this weightlessness is achieved in 30-second periods as a large jet airplane dives from 34,000 feet to 24,000 feet dozens of times in a day. Pilot astronauts maintain their flying proficiency by flying at least 15 hours a month in NASA trainer jets.

The astronauts begin their formal space transportation system training by reading manuals and by taking computer-based training lessons on the various space orbiter systems. Next, they work in the single systems trainer, where each astronaut is accompanied by an instructor who helps him or her learn about the operations of each orbiter subsystem using checklists similar to those used on an actual mission.

Following that part of the training, astronauts begin working in the complex shuttle mission simulators (SMS's). This is where they are trained in all areas of shuttle vehicle operations and systems tasks associated with major space flights: from prelaunch and ascent to orbit operations, entry, and landing. The orbit training includes payload operation, payload deployment and retrieval, maneuvers and rendezvous. In the simulators, a digital image-generation system depicts the visual images the astronauts will see throughout their mission—the Earth, stars, payloads, the landing runway. In other words, a space shuttle mission is simulated from launch to landing.

Once astronauts are assigned to a particular mission—usually about 10 months before the flight—they begin training on computer software similar to that to be used on the flight. They get the actual flight software for training about 11 weeks before their mission. During those last 11 weeks, the astronauts also train with the flight controllers at the Mission Control Center. Their training facility is linked to the center the same way the space-craft and center are linked during an actual mission. This way the astronauts and controllers learn to work as a team, solving problems and working out procedures and timelines for particular activities of that mission.

Another weightless environment astronauts train in is a huge water tank that contains a mock-up of the shuttle orbiter pay-load bay and various payloads. Payload is the things carried by the spacecraft (passengers, instruments) that are directly related to the purpose of the flight (as opposed to things needed for operation—such as fuel). Under water the astronauts wear space suits (extravehicular mobility units) that are made neutrally buoyant. This reduces the sensation of gravity and provides a very close simulation of the actual working environment in space.

The astronauts also practice space mission tasks—ranging from meal preparation and trash management to the use of cameras and equipment stowage—in several full-scale mock- ups and trainers. They also participate in test and checkout activities at the NASA Kennedy Space Center in Florida, from where space shuttles are launched.

The months of preparation pay off in the high degree of mission success. Actual missions usually have far fewer contin-gencies than the astronauts practiced for. Astronauts have commented that only the noise and vibration of the liftoff and launch of the shuttle and the actual prolonged experience of weightlessness are missing from the practice sessions; ev-erything else in training accurately duplicates the real space experience.

Even after the orbiter returns to earth, the astronauts' mission continues. The crew spends several days in debriefing, where they recount their experiences for the benefit of future crews and trainers. Then, after a brief vacation, they resume their studies and training that may eventually lead to another space flight assignment.

Getting into NASA

There are basically three astronaut specialties you can apply for: commander/pilot, mission specialist, or payload specialist.

Commander/pilot astronauts serve as both space shuttle commanders and pilots. During flight, the commander has full responsibility for the spacecraft, crew, mission success, and safety of the flight. The pilot assists the commander in controlling and operating the vehicle and may assist in deploying and retrieving satellites using the remote manipulator system—the robot arm that operates out of the payload bay of the shuttle orbiter.

Mission specialist astronauts have overall responsibility for coordinating shuttle operations in the following areas: crew activity planning, consumables usage, and experiment/payload operations. They are trained in the details of the orbiter on-board systems and in the operational characteristics, requirements and objectives, and supporting equipment and systems for each of the space experiments to be conducted on the mission. Mission specialists also perform EVA's—extravehicular activities, or space walks. Now that's a trip!

Payload specialists are persons other than NASA astronauts who have specialized on-board duties. They may be foreign nationals. They may be added to shuttle crews if activities with unique requirements are involved in the mission and more than the minimum crew of five persons is needed. First consideration for these additional crew members is given to qualified NASA mission specialists. And when payload specialists are required, they are nominated by NASA, the foreign sponsor, or the designated payload sponsor. Although payload specialists are not part of the astronaut program, they must have the appropriate education and training needed for the payload experiment and must pass NASA space physical exams.

NASA accepts applications for the Astronaut Candidate Program on a continuous basis. Candidates are selected as needed for pilot and mission specialist slots. Normally the selection is made every two years. Civilians and military personnel may apply.

To qualify for training as either a pilot or a mission specialist astronaut, you must have at least a bachelor's degree in engineering, biological or physical science, or mathematics, plus three years of related, progressively responsible professional experience. An advanced degree is desirable and may be substituted for all or part of the experience requirement.

Pilot astronauts must also have at least a thousand hours pilot-in-command time in jet aircraft (flight test experience is highly desirable). They must pass a NASA Class I space physical, which is similar to a military or civilian Class I flight physical, and be between 64 and 76 inches tall. Mission specialists must pass a NASA Class II space physical, which allows a slightly lower level of visual acuity.

Applicants who meet the basic qualifications are evaluated during a week-long process of personal interviews, medical exams, and orientation. Because several hundred applicants fulfill the basic requirements, the final selection is based largely on personal interviews. Astronauts are expected to be team players and highly skilled generalists with just the right amount of individuality and self-reliance to be effective crew members.

Applicants who are selected are designated astronaut candidates and are assigned to the astronaut office at the Johnson Space Center for a one-year training and evaluation period during which they are assigned technical or scientific responsibilities and participate in training designed to develop the knowledge and skills required for formal mission training upon selection for a flight. Your selection as a full-fledged astronaut is based on satisfactory completion of the one-year program. Civilian candidates who are selected as astronauts are expected to remain with NASA for at least five years; military astronauts are detailed to NASA for a specified tour of duty by their branch of the armed forces.

Your Future as an Astronaut

In the 1990s the space shuttle will continue to be NASA's workhorse vehicle for hauling people and cargo into Earth's orbit. There are more than 60 missions scheduled through 1995. That's the year when the NASA master plan calls for shuttle crews to begin constructing a permanent orbiting base in the sky—space station Freedom.

Astronauts aboard Freedom will perform virtually every space activity that humans can conceive of. The station will supplant the shuttle as an orbiting laboratory for microgravity experiments in fluid dynamics, production of new and improved metals and alloys and biotechnology research. Crews will investigate the medical effects of long duration stays in zero gravity and test new robotic technology.

As the space station takes shape, engineers and scientists will continue to plan new ways to get humans and their equipment into orbit. Eventually astronauts may ride into space aboard new space planes. And for the first time in years, NASA is looking beyond Earth's orbit to a new era of adventure in space. Early in the twenty-first century, the plan is to send Americans to the Moon again. From bases on the Moon, manned voyages to Mars and other parts of the universe will be launched.

For travel buffs, this must be the most promising career of all.

Salaries for civilian astronauts are based on the federal government's General Schedule pay scales. For astronauts these pay scales range from grades GS-11 ($31,116–$40,449 a year) through GS-14 ($52,406–$68,129) depending on the individual's education and experience. Military astronauts, of course, are paid by their service branch according to their rank and time in service.

For more information:
For a pilot and mission specialist astronaut application package, write to:

Astronaut Selection Office
Mail Code AHX
Johnson Space Center
Houston, TX 77058

For information about opportunities as a payload specialist, write to:

NASA Headquarters
Attn: Code OST-5
Washington, DC 20546

Job Hunting

A s a practical matter, finding a job that involves travel calls for the same techniques and strategy you would use to search for any kind of job. But being a travel buff may give you an edge in some cases because for many people business travel is not at all attractive. Indeed, they may avoid jobs that require traveling.

Conducting a job search is a hard job that requires a lot of skill, enterprise, and energy. And most people aren't very good at it. It's no wonder, because most of us go through the process of looking for a job only sporadically in our working lifetimes. A reasonably successful person might change jobs only six or seven times in 35 years of work.

So since this task is probably somewhat foreign to you, take the time to study it before you dive in. There are dozens of books on how to conduct a successful job search; get one, and read through it. Here are some of the tips you're likely to find in most job-hunting books:

Lay the groundwork for your search. Compose a resume that presents a comprehensive, but quick survey of your experience and accomplishments. Try to keep it to a page, two at most. Your resume doesn't have to detail your life history; its purpose is to get you in the door at a company—to get you invited to an interview. You don't get jobs from resumes. You can only get a job from an interview.

In order to get those interviews, you'll have to do some research on the employment scene in your community, or beyond if you aren't adverse to moving away. Consult business directories and other resources at your local library for names of companies and other organizations that have the kinds of jobs you seek. Get names of appropriate managers at those companies, then write to them about a job. Also check the help-wanted ads in your local newspaper and in journals and publications in your professional field.

Practice for those interviews. Get a friend to act as an employer and interview you, so you can figure out how to react to different questions and situations. Common sense will tell you a lot about how to handle an interview—be on time, dressed for business, and well groomed. Bone up on the company before you go for the interview, so you'll be able to ask some intelligent questions and respond knowledgeably to the interviewer's inquiries. Don't argue with the interviewer. Don't badmouth other employers or jobs. Take with you samples of your work and other materials an employer might want to see.

The real key is to be relaxed and comfortable with the situation. If you are, the back-and-forth exchange between you and the interviewer will probably be quite conversational—normal—and that will demonstrate that you interact well with other people. And communicating well is a major criterion for any job.

Network. Tell everyone you know that you are looking for a job. You never can tell when one of them may hear of something and let you know. That's how many people find their jobs—through word of mouth and networking among friends and business colleagues. Follow up every lead you get about a job, even if it doesn't sound all that promising at first. At the very least, it may give you a chance to practice your interview technique. And, if you're lucky, it could turn out to be the job of your dreams.

Persevere. Finding a job can take time. The high
the job and the pay, the longer it can take. I
discouraged when you don't get calls you hoped f
your inquiries. But keep your spirits up. Eventu
who wants a job finds one. Landing the particular
where you get to travel, may take longer than you
you may have to take a circuitous course—fo
accepting a different, but related job in order to b
to move into the job you really want at a later tin

As a travel buff, when you find that perfect jot
have been worth it. Good luck with your search
lets you travel!

Persevere. Finding a job can take time. The higher the level of the job and the pay, the longer it can take. It's easy to get discouraged when you don't get calls you hoped for or replies to your inquiries. But keep your spirits up. Eventually everybody who wants a job finds one. Landing the particular job you want, where you get to travel, may take longer than you thought. And you may have to take a circuitous course—for instance, by accepting a different, but related job in order to be in a position to move into the job you really want at a later time.

As a travel buff, when you find that perfect job, the wait will have been worth it. Good luck with your search for a job that lets you travel!

interview. You don't get jobs from resumes. You can only get a job from an interview.

In order to get those interviews, you'll have to do some research on the employment scene in your community, or beyond if you aren't adverse to moving away. Consult business directories and other resources at your local library for names of companies and other organizations that have the kinds of jobs you seek. Get names of appropriate managers at those companies, then write to them about a job. Also check the help-wanted ads in your local newspaper and in journals and publications in your professional field.

Practice for those interviews. Get a friend to act as an employer and interview you, so you can figure out how to react to different questions and situations. Common sense will tell you a lot about how to handle an interview—be on time, dressed for business, and well groomed. Bone up on the company before you go for the interview, so you'll be able to ask some intelligent questions and respond knowledgeably to the interviewer's inquiries. Don't argue with the interviewer. Don't badmouth other employers or jobs. Take with you samples of your work and other materials an employer might want to see.

The real key is to be relaxed and comfortable with the situation. If you are, the back-and-forth exchange between you and the interviewer will probably be quite conversational—normal—and that will demonstrate that you interact well with other people. And communicating well is a major criterion for any job.

Network. Tell everyone you know that you are looking for a job. You never can tell when one of them may hear of something and let you know. That's how many people find their jobs—through word of mouth and networking among friends and business colleagues. Follow up every lead you get about a job, even if it doesn't sound all that promising at first. At the very least, it may give you a chance to practice your interview technique. And, if you're lucky, it could turn out to be the job of your dreams.